GROUNDSWELL

THE MUSEUM OF MODERN ART, NEW YORK

Peter Reed

GROUNDSWELL

constructing

the

contemporary landscape

Published on the occasion of the exhibition *Groundswell: Constructing the Contemporary Landscape*, February 25–May 16, 2005, at The Museum of Modern Art, New York, organized by Peter Reed, Curator, Department of Architecture and Design.

The exhibition is the third in a series of five exhibitions made possible by The Lily Auchincloss Fund for Contemporary Architecture.

Additional support is provided by the Estate of Florene M. Schoenborn, Patricia Phelps de Cisneros, and the Evelyn and Walter Haas, Jr. Fund.

The accompanying publication is made possible by Elise Jaffe + Jeffrey Brown, the Blanchette Hooker Rockefeller Fund, and Furthermore: a program of the J. M. Kaplan Fund.

The accompanying educational programs are made possible by BNP Paribas.

Produced by the Department of Publications, The Museum of Modern Art, New York
Edited by Libby Hruska
Designed by Amanda Washburn
Production by Christina Grillo

Printed and bound by Dr. Cantz'sche Druckerei, Ostfildern, Germany
Typeset in Locator and DIN
Printed on 150 gsm ProfiMatt

Printed in Germany

Library of Congress Control Number: 2004117647

Published by
The Museum of Modern Art
11 West 53 Street
New York, NY 10019-5497
www.moma.org

Distributed in the United States and Canada by D.A.P./Distributed Art Publishers, Inc., New York
www.artbook.com

Distributed outside the United States, Canada, Germany, Austria, and Switzerland by Thames & Hudson, Ltd, London
www.thameshudson.co.uk

Distributed in Germany, Austria, and Switzerland by Birkhäuser – Publishers for Architecture
Basel • Berlin • Boston
www.birkhauser.ch

MoMA ISBN: 0-87070-379-X

Thames & Hudson ISBN: 0-87070-379-X

Birkhäuser ISBN: 3-7643-7240-0

Front cover: Clockwise from top left: Mosbach Paysagistes, Bordeaux Botanical Garden; Martha Schwartz, Inc., Exchange Square; Latz + Partner, Duisburg-Nord Landscape Park; Paysage Land and Valode & Pistre Architectes, Shell Petroleum Headquarters; Hargreaves Associates, Crissy Field; West 8 urban design & landscape architecture bv, Schouwburgplein (Theater Square)

Back cover: Clockwise from top: Field Operations, Fresh Kills *lifescape*; West 8 urban design & landscape architecture bv, Schouwburgplein (Theater Square); OHTORI Consultants Environmental Design Institute, Peter Walker William Johnson and Partners, and NTT Urban Development Co., Keyaki Plaza; Tom Leader Studio, Shanghai Carpet

Inside cover: Ken Smith Landscape Architect, The Museum of Modern Art Roof Garden. Plan of South Garden

Page 3: Enric Miralles and Carme Pinós, Igualada Cemetery Park

Page 4: Clockwise from top left: Hargreaves Associates, Crissy Field; ARUP and EDAW, Piccadilly Gardens; Tom Leader Studio, Shanghai Carpet

Page 5: Clockwise from top left: Latz + Partner, Duisburg-Nord Landscape Park; Atelier Phusis, Invalidenpark; Field Operations, Fresh Kills *lifescape*

Page 6: Paysage Land and Valode & Pistre Architectes, Shell Petroleum Headquarters; OHTORI Consultants Environmental Design Institute, Peter Walker William Johnson and Partners, and NTT Urban Development Co., Keyaki Plaza

Page 7: West 8 urban design & landscape architecture bv, Schouwburgplein (Theater Square)

Page 10: Desvigne & Dalnoky, Greenwich Peninsula

CONTENTS

FOREWORD

When The Museum of Modern Art opened its first permanent building in 1939 it included an outdoor sculpture garden, generally considered to be one of the first attempts to build such a space according to modernist principles of design. Alfred H. Barr, Jr., the Museum's founding director, and John McAndrew, curator of architecture, designed this pioneering garden. Ever since, the garden—brilliantly redesigned in the early 1950s by Philip Johnson—has been the centerpiece of the Museum's campus. Around the time the first garden opened to the public, the young Museum's Architecture Committee envisioned that modern landscape design would be included in the exhibition program so that significant developments in the design of outdoor environments would be brought to the public's attention.

Although the ambition was not reflected in the Museum's programs with the same intensity as architecture and industrial design, several noteworthy episodes stand out. The first was the publication of Elizabeth B. Kassler's *Modern Gardens and the Landscape* in 1964 (republished in 1984). For years it remained one of the few surveys of the field. In 1991, the Museum presented *Roberto Burle Marx: The Unnatural Art of the Garden*, an exhibition that highlighted the life work of the Brazilian landscape architect, foremost among the creators of an influential modern landscape aesthetic.

Since the early 1990s the surge of creative activity in contemporary landscape design is evidenced by the fast pace with which cities are reclaiming sites and transforming them into new and compellingly beautiful public spaces. The design of constructed landscapes has gained a new relevance in our postindustrial era, coupled with a greater appreciation that the design of spaces between buildings is as critical to the quality of our urban environment as the buildings themselves. *Groundswell: Constructing the Contemporary Landscape*, organized by Peter Reed, Curator, Department of Architecture and Design, with the assistance of Irene Shum, Curatorial Assistant, presents an international survey that reflects the artistic richness and many of the critical issues confronting designers working in this milieu today. Rather than focus on a single typology, *Groundswell* presents a range of projects—from small urban plazas and gardens to large parks built in such inhospitable environments as former steelworks and sanitary landfills. Some of these projects blur conventional distinctions between architecture, engineering, and landscape, underscoring the complexity of constructed landscapes, particularly in the urban realm. Landscapes, like cities, evolve and change over time in response to nature's processes and to human needs. The transformations shown here not only reflect the creative talent of today's designers but are ultimately a measure of how cultures value and use open spaces.

Groundswell: Constructing the Contemporary Landscape is the third in a series of five exhibitions made possible by The Lily Auchincloss Fund for Contemporary Architecture, which is named in honor of Lily Auchincloss, Trustee of The Museum of Modern Art from 1971 to 1996 and Chairman of the Museum's Committee on Architecture and Design from 1981 to 1995. The previous exhibitions, *The Un-Private House* (1999) and *Tall Buildings* (2004), organized by Terence Riley, the Philip Johnson Chief Curator of Architecture and Design, who conceived the series, focused on individual building types. The Museum is grateful for the additional support from Patricia Phelps de Cisneros, Trustee and Chairman of the Committee on Architecture and Design, and from the Evelyn and Walter Haas, Jr. Fund. This publication received support from Elise Jaffe and Jeffrey Brown, the Blanchette Hooker Rockefeller Fund, and Furthermore: a program of the J. M. Kaplan Fund. These individuals and foundations share a keen interest in and commitment to focusing our attention on contemporary projects that engage all aspects of architecture and design. Finally, I am particularly grateful to Peter Reed, who conceived and organized this exhibition and whose passionate interest in contemporary landscape design is matched only by the sharpness of his mind and the depth of his understanding of the built environment.

Glenn D. Lowry
Director, The Museum of Modern Art

ACKNOWLEDGMENTS

The seeds for this project were planted nearly a decade ago when I became aware of the innovative work taking place in contemporary landscape design, especially in the public realm. I vividly recall lectures by landscape architects, including Adriaan Geuze, Peter Latz, Martha Schwartz, and Ken Smith, in various forums presented by The Architectural League of New York. Their extraordinary and imaginative designs stimulated my innate interests in the art of landscape, urban design, and public spaces. My initial explorations in this field were enriched and broadened by the many practitioners, historians, and critics I met in recent years at symposia at Harvard University's Graduate School of Design, the University of Pennsylvania's School of Design, and in our own educational programs at the Museum presented jointly with colleagues at the Van Alen Institute. In 1997 I initially proposed an exhibition on the subject of contemporary landscape design to the Museum, and from the beginning the project has been wholeheartedly supported by Glenn Lowry, Director, and Terence Riley, the Philip Johnson Chief Curator of Architecture and Design.

On behalf of the Museum I would like to express our gratitude to the many architects and landscape architects whose work is included in this exhibition. Their passion and creativity remained a major source of inspiration throughout the project, and they generously devoted time and resources to discuss their work with me and to produce materials for the catalogue and exhibition. I would also like to acknowledge key members of their staffs who worked with us for many months: Christof Brinkmann and Pablo Martínez Capdevila of Abalos & Herreros; Greg Bussien of ADR; David West, former director of Alsop Big, Alsop Ltd; Ana Marti-Baron, Sophie Mourthé, and Pauline Way for Michel Desvigne; Juli Grot and Paula Garvey of EDAW, as well as principals Joe Brown and Jason Prior; Ellen Neises of Field Operations; Stefan Hoerner and Pablo Ros of Foreign Office Architects; Yael Ifrah for Christophe Girot; Jeanne Ernst for Kathryn Gustafson; Cass Salzwedel of Gustafson Guthrie Nichol Ltd.; Mary Bowman, Kinna Stallard, and Max Norman of Gustafson Porter Ltd; Megan Mann, Eamin Tobin, and Stephanie McCullough of Hargreaves Associates; Anneliese Latz of Latz + Partner; Jennifer Mui of Mosbach Paysagistes; Miho Kawamura of OHTORI Consultants Environmental Design Institute; Flora Muñoz for Carme Pinós; Lynn M. Dermody of Martha Schwartz, Inc.; Elizabeth Asawa of Ken Smith Landscape Architect; James Lord of Peter Walker and Partners, Landscape Architecture, Inc.; Yehre Suh of Weiss/Manfredi Architects; and Fanny Smelik of West 8 urban design & landscape architecture bv.

In addition to the designers who loaned models and other materials for the exhibition, I am grateful for the cooperation and generosity of other lenders for permitting the Museum to exhibit models from their collections: ADR and the City of Paris; Maud Marshall, Chief Executive, Bradford Centre Regeneration; Antonio Beaus, General Director, Ecoparc del Mediterrani; Benedetta Tagliabue, EMBT Arquitectes Associats; Mimi Gardner Gates, Director, and Chris Rogers, Director of Capital Projects, Seattle Art Museum; and Angus Gavin, Urban Development Division Manager, Solidere, The Lebanese Company for the Development and Reconstruction of Beirut Central District, s.a.l. I would also like to acknowledge the talented individuals who produced new videos of landscapes in an effort to bring these sites to life in the context of the exhibition: Valéry Didelon for Bordeaux Botanical Garden; David Donnenfield of David Donnenfield Productions for Crissy Field; Justine and Alex Heilner of Field Operations for Fresh Kills *lifescape*; video artist Marc Schwartz for Invalidenpark; David Lloyd and Dixi Carillo of EDAW for all three projects in Manchester, England; Chris Hoxie and Brandon Hicks of BHCH, LLC, for the animation of the Seattle Art Museum's Olympic Sculpture Park; and Hans Werlemann of Hectic Pictures for Schouwburgplein.

As with every exhibition in which I have been involved at the Museum, my colleagues in various departments have proved to be talented, dedicated, and encouraging. Michael Margitich, Deputy Director, External Affairs; Todd Bishop, Director, Exhibition Funding; and Mary Hannah, Assistant Director, Exhibition Funding, make it possible for curators to dream. Those dreams are brought to life with the assistance of a large team, which for

Groundswell included: Jennifer Russell, Deputy Director of Exhibitions; Maria DeMarco Beardsley, Coordinator of Exhibitions; Randolph Black, Associate Coordinator of Exhibitions; Heidi O'Neill, Senior Assistant Registrar; Lynda Zycherman, Conservator; Stephen Clark, Associate General Counsel; Nancy Adelson, Assistant General Counsel; Deborah Schwartz, Deputy Director for Education; Sarah Ganz, Director, Educational Resources; David Little, Director, Adult and Academic Programs; Laura Beiles, Assistant Educator, Adult and Academic Programs; Kim Mitchell, Director of Communications; and Matthew Montgomery, Senior Publicist. I would also like to extend thanks to Sarah Hermanson Meister, Associate Curator, Collections and Research, Department of Photography, and Jennifer Tobias, Librarian, Collection Development, who greatly assisted our research.

The exhibition installation could not have been realized without the talent, cooperation, and insightful understanding of Jerome Neuner, Director of Exhibition Design and Production, and his assistant, Lana Hum, Exhibition Designer/Production Manager. Kate Johnson, Senior Designer, and Claire Corey, Production Manager, both in the Department of Graphic Design, gave the exhibition its graphic identity and produced a wide range of materials in conjunction with the show. In the Department of Digital Media, Allegra Burnette, Creative Manager, and Maggie D'Errico, Senior Producer, assisted with web design and special presentations for the exhibition, and Charles Kalinowski, Manager of Audiovisual Services, and his colleagues coordinated the display of new media.

The Department of Publications, under the leadership of Michael Maegraith, Publisher, deserves resounding applause for producing this catalogue to its unwavering professional standards during a particularly hectic period at the Museum. Libby Hruska, Associate Editor, brought insight and clarity to the texts with characteristic scrutiny. Amanda Washburn, Senior Book Designer, and Christina Grillo, Associate Production Manager, designed and produced a beautiful publication that reflects a sensitive understanding of the material.

Several colleagues in the Department of Architecture and Design worked closely with me, including Jane Tschang, Year-Long Intern, who assisted with research on specific projects and the field of contemporary landscape in general, and Christine Canabou, Intern, and Tina diCarlo, Assistant Curator, who assisted with photo research. I would also like to thank Kanitra Fletcher, Department Assistant, Rachel Judlowe, Coordinator, and Curbie Oestreich, Manager, for their administrative assistance. Irene Shum, Curatorial Assistant, is a valued colleague and deserves special mention. Irene joined the Museum specifically to work on this project, and her insights, informed opinions, hard work, and good humor are reflected in all aspects of the project.

Lastly, I would like to extend my personal thanks to Elise Jaffe and Jeffrey Brown for their many years of friendship and for committing their support to this publication early on, as did Joan Davidson, whose remarkable foundation, Furthermore, also supported the book. I find their interests in all things architectural to be engaging and an inspiration.

Peter Reed
Curator, Department of Architecture and Design

VIEW FROM THE FORT, NEAR BRISTOL.

BEYOND BEFORE AND AFTER

designing

contemporary landscape

PETER REED

VIEW FROM THE FORT, NEAR BRISTOL.

LANDSCAPES ARE MADE AND REMADE. The works in this exhibition are primarily new urban public landscapes that did not exist as public space half a generation ago. Nearly every significant new landscape designed in recent years occupies a site that has been reinvented and reclaimed from obsolescence or degradation as cities in the postindustrial era remake and redefine their outdoor spaces. In the early 1980s a visitor to what is now Duisburg-Nord Landscape Park in Germany's rust-belt would have found an active steelworks. In Beirut's city center, a public garden is being built where civil war raged. In central Rotterdam a public square routinely co-opted as a parking lot has been reimagined as a town square and gathering place. *Groundswell: Constructing the Contemporary Landscape* portrays the surge of creativity and critical commentary surrounding the contemporary created landscape by presenting a diverse selection of plazas, public parks, and urban sectors that have recently been completed or are in the process of being realized. The survey reveals the diverse ways that cities confront change by revaluing and reprogramming their spaces, ranging from a small urban square created in the aftermath of a terrorist bombing to the daunting task of transforming America's largest landfill—where as much as 29,000 tons of garbage was dumped daily—into a wildlife sanctuary and place for recreation. The formal diversity in these designs reflects not only the individual designer's aesthetic and theoretical ideas about landscape—an art of horizontal surfaces and systems, impermanence and change—but also the way a design responds to the site, the most fundamental phenomenon underlying constructed landscapes.

The projects discussed here illustrate many kinds of sites, a multivalent term that includes the physical properties of the ground, its history, and program for the new landscape. Innovative reinterpretations of the traditional town square—including roof gardens and plazas designed on top of underground parking garages—are common examples of artificially constructed surfaces that present opportunities for new public amenities, often coupled with a desire to conceal what lies below ground. Designers also explore the relationship between artifice and nature by sculpting new topographies that are inspired by natural environments. Perhaps the most pervasive landscapes encountered in our postindustrial era, however, are abused and polluted sites that present numerous challenges, ranging from the remediation of toxic environments to defining new programs for these inhospitable places. In some instances pollution can be capped and hidden from view. Elsewhere the ground is so toxic that all soil must be removed. The result is a kind of tabula rasa, which has led some to seek a more distant nature that once occupied the site while others find opportunities to construct new landforms. Sites can also suffer from what one might call cultural pollution: places profoundly affected by human strife and civil unrest. In remaking these landscapes the question of whether to reveal or conceal the traces of a site's history—whether natural, industrial, or political—defines its genius loci and ultimately plays a role in the form, meaning, and cultural significance of the new design.

No matter what the approach, the transformations are often spectacular. One of the best ways to appreciate these changes—some of which are slow and gradual—is through images of before and after. The juxtaposition of such images is an old device in landscape, made famous by Humphrey Repton, the late-eighteenth- and early-nineteenth-century British landscape designer. Repton presented his clients with so-called Red Books (named for their red leather binding) in which a hinged overlay demonstrated the improvements to an otherwise dull scene. In a pair of renderings for a house known as the Fort, Repton illustrated the improved prospect from the house by proposing a dense screen of trees and

shrubs to conceal a new development of unsightly row houses in the distance (figs. 1 and 2). In the foreground, he transformed an abandoned building site, which had left a gaping hole in the ground and mounds of earth, by reshaping the ground and softening the contours. The resulting view was more attractive and more suitable to its role as a public recreation ground, which it had already become in Repton's time. For Repton, the overlay was a clever sales technique. When applied to the projects discussed here, the juxtaposition of before and after is intended to elucidate the work of contemporary designers by illustrating the range of conditions they confront as they remake landscapes to serve new programs and constituencies. To be sure, Repton's device has its shortcomings in that it reduces landscape design to an exercise in "picture-making" without describing the fullness of the processes. Designers today are especially aware of the complexities of landscape design, such as growth and change, that cannot be fixed in a single picture. Moreover, landscape has the ability to connect the past, present, and future. The sense of time and process that sees landscape in an ever-present state of becoming is relevant to all projects and may affect the way a designer visualizes a site's spatial and temporal qualities.[1]

The reinvention and remediation of the sites surveyed here are a measure of artistic creativity and of our changing aesthetic sensibilities and attitudes toward natural and man-made environments. They also reflect landscape's expanded field of activity that variously engages urban planning, engineering, and architecture, as designers give shape to inert and living materials, rich in textures and colors, and enhanced by light and water to create meaningful spaces. These parks and plazas not only provide a connection to nature, they are also places for social interaction, recreation, for unimagined and unanticipated activities, and, thankfully, places to do nothing. Because of the role public space plays as a catalyst for urban development and in the quality of civic life, how these palliative spaces are treated is ultimately a reflection of our culture. As such the constructed landscapes included here are causes for optimism.

DESIGNING THE URBAN STAGE

The town square is one of the most traditional types of urban public space. The piazza, village green, and other kinds of "outdoor rooms" are in many ways the locus of public life. They are social spaces, places to gather, to meet, and simply an alternative to being indoors. They take their identity as much from the surrounding architecture as from the design of the spaces themselves. Among the projects included here are plazas for new urban developments and significant refurbishments of spaces that had lost their civic value. For each project the designers have endeavored to create a unique visual and symbolic identity by various means, such as the selection of materials, trees, and plants with meaningful associations, iconographical elements, and the recovery of historical traces.

Rotterdam's Schouwburgplein (Theater Square) (pp. 34–39), designed by Adriaan Geuze of West 8, is an ingenious reinterpretation of the traditional town square. Much of central Rotterdam was bombed in World War II and the planning and architecture that characterized the rebuilding resulted in uninspired spaces. Before Geuze's intervention the square lacked a sense of place and had frequently been co-opted as a parking lot, much to the public's chagrin. The new design, constructed on top of an underground parking garage, needed to signal that this was a car-free zone. To give this square its unique identity Geuze drew references from Rotterdam's port—the largest in Europe. Schouwburgplein is a vast open deck set three steps above the surrounding streets. Geuze's simple gesture of elevating the deck ensured that the square would remain a pedestrian preserve. Circumstances dictated that the surface be lightweight, which precluded planting, but the raised deck provided an interstitial space for infrastructure elements such as lighting and fountains. The platform is constructed of an amalgam of materials with varying textures and timbers, evident as one traverses the square: wood boardwalk, perforated steel plates and grates, rubber, and smooth epoxy embedded with maple leaves. To make the reference to the port fully explicit, a map is etched on the surface. Aligned along one edge of the flat square are a single row of benches and the square's principal icons: towering machinelike light masts painted bright red that were inspired by industrial cranes for lifting cargo. These articulated structures cast pools of light on the square.

In addition to being a compelling formal exercise in material and meaning, Geuze also considers Schouwburgplein to be a polemical statement on the role of public space in contemporary urban culture. He saw little need to impose a program on the design of this public stage, believing that people will use the space in unpredictable ways. Geuze considers his countrymen in Holland, Europe's most densely populated country, to be too restricted in their activities and in need of places for emotional release: "The users of a space should be actors, not spectators...the public spaces in cities and the countryside drain users of their intelligence—people are always following signs and being told what to do."[2] Dutch critic Bart Lootsma places Geuze's argument in context: "According to Geuze this neglected but very lively landscape holds the seeds of the future European city, in which the inhabitants no longer need illusions or stopgaps, but define their own exotic culture. Their behaviour can or need no longer be preprogrammed since it is based on anarchy, exploration and self-expression."[3] In this respect Geuze may have been inspired by the competition held for Parc de la Villette in Paris in 1982, some years before he began his practice, that emphasized program over design. In an essay about park design, Geuze noted that the modern park was "no longer seen as a quiet rural green area, but as a sparkling and overcharged urban crossroads. Instead of a product produced by automatic pilot, the park was linked anew to the aspirations of the urban society."[4] At Schouwburgplein, the spotlights from the light masts underscore the notion of the town square as stage where roller bladers, kids playing in fountains, temporary markets, crowds coming to the nearby theaters, and people partaking of myriad other activities assume their roles.

The city of Manchester, England, has also recognized the vital role public space can play as a catalyst and magnet for urban development. In 1996, when Manchester was rocked by a devastating IRA bombing, the city seized the opportunity to revitalize its damaged center. It chose EDAW's master plan to do so (pp. 40–41).[5] In addition to restoring and rebuilding the industrial center's architectural fabric the plan emphasizes an improved network of roads, pedestrian paths, and public areas. The city's principal open spaces—the recently refurbished Piccadilly Gardens, centrally located at the nexus of many transportation routes, and the new Exchange Square—now cast the city in a contemporary light. Like Schouwburgplein, Piccadilly Gardens (pp. 48–51) was completely redesigned and reconceived as the city's active public stage, something Manchester did not previously have. A tired, traffic-choked nineteenth-century park was replaced with a bold, minimalist design by ARUP and EDAW as the city's new gathering space. Far more accessible than the old park, people are drawn to the large elliptical fountain and the paths and so-called catwalk that traverse the park. The wide-open spaces and fountain are framed by Tadao Ando's arcing concrete pavilion—the Japanese architect's first work in Britain. The contemporary design of the park and its architecture are intended to signal Manchester's progressive spirit and a vibrant core.

Several blocks from Piccadilly, Martha Schwartz's Exchange Square (pp. 42–47) replaced a tangled intersection in the commercial heart of Manchester near the epicenter of the bomb. The new space, intended to accommodate the large crowds that congregate in this bustling commercial district, presented little opportunity for planting. Schwartz designed a hard-surface plaza, punctuated with a few stands of birch trees, that combines a lively composition with references to Manchester's history. The visual tension in the contrasting paving patterns—horizontal stripes counterpoised with the concentric arcing curves of ramps and benches that brilliantly negotiate a sloping site—suits the push and pull in this commercial district. The design reflects the city's ambition to create a new contemporary public space, and it evinces Schwartz's exploration of geometric forms in the landscape inspired by Minimalist art. Schwartz and her former partner, Peter Walker, both share an interest in the work of artists such as Carl Andre, Al Held, Frank Stella, and others, who employed geometry and repetition in their work as a means of organizing space and evoking a range of emotions. For Schwartz, the gritty urban environment provides particularly appropriate sites for exploring the relationship between geometry and the landscape: "Simple geometric forms, such as circles and squares, are familiar and memorable images.... Simple geometries are thus best used in the landscape as mental maps. Given the nature of our built environment, the use of geometry in the landscape is more humane than the disorientation caused by the incessant lumps, bumps and squiggles of a stylized naturalism. Geometry allows us to recognize and place ourselves in space and is more formally sympathetic to architecture. Lastly, it deals with our manufactured environments more honestly; geometry itself is a rational construct and thereby avoids the issue of trying to mask our man-made environments with a thin veneer of naturalism."[6]

Juxtaposed to the universalizing abstract patterns, Schwartz introduced a number of specific elements that more explicitly refer to Manchester's industrial and historic heritage. The intricate rough stonework of the Hanging Ditch fountain, which cuts across the lower edge of the square, traces a historic waterway that had long been paved over. In a more lighthearted vein, stylized railcars with bright blue benches set on tracks and the proposed artificial palm trees impart a Pop element characteristic of the humor and occasional irreverence found throughout Schwartz's work. Like the Pop artists she also admires, Schwartz is drawn to banal, everyday objects as reflections of our common culture and for their ability to "illuminate the stuff of our everyday lives."[7]

FIG. 3: DAN KILEY. RIVERSIDE PARK,
NATIONSBANK (FORMERLY NORTH CAROLINA
NATIONAL BANK) PLAZA, TAMPA, 1988

FIG. 4: CARL ANDRE. *144 LEAD SQUARES*. 1969. ⅜" x 12' x 12'
(1 x 366 x 366 CM). THE MUSEUM OF MODERN ART, NEW YORK.
ADVISORY COMMITTEE FUND, 1969

FIG. 5: PETER WALKER WITH THE SWA GROUP.
CAMBRIDGE CENTER ROOF GARDEN,
CAMBRIDGE, MASSACHUSSETTS, 1979

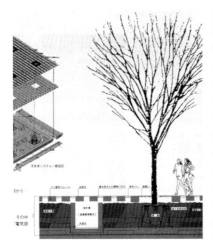

FIG. 6: PETER WALKER, PETER WALKER WILLIAM
JOHNSON AND PARTNERS; YOJI SASAKI, OHTORI
CONSULTANTS ENVIRONMENTAL DESIGN
INSTITUTE; MASAYUKI KUSUMOTO, NTT URBAN
DEVELOPMENT CO. KEYAKI PLAZA, SAITAMA
NEW URBAN CENTER, SAITAMA CITY, JAPAN,
1994–2000. SECTION OF THE ARTIFICIAL SUBSOIL
SYSTEM

pletely controlling the character and nature of the 'empty' space above."[13] The nonhierarchical composition, the repetitive module, and flat ground became hallmarks of Walker's designs, especially those built on rooftops. His Cambridge Center Roof Garden of 1979 was among the first such projects with modular patterned materials and stylized abstract "trees" in the manner of LeWitt sculptures (fig. 5).

Designers have long responded to the often unremarkable and restrictive site conditions of building on slab with significant, beautiful landscapes. This modernist conceit recalls Le Corbusier's "Five Points Toward a New Architecture," written in 1926, wherein he claimed the roof garden as a principal means of bringing nature into the urban environment in the form of an outdoor room. Walker and Sasaki have described Keyaki Plaza as metaphorically transporting a piece of ground from the shrine and making it the building's fifth elevation, open to the sky. Keyaki's modular design, with its grid pattern of alternating stone and perforated metal panels, establishes a formal congruence with the geometries of the building's curtain wall. Under the plaza's paved surface Walker and Sasaki constructed a kind of hydroponic "earth room" that is revealed in section and is visible as a dark linear stripe along the building's facades (fig. 6).[14] The designers have engineered an outdoor plaza that is wholly artificial yet simulates natural processes.

Because the plaza's ground plane is truly flat—rather than pitched at an imperceptible grade like most roof gardens—it allows water to percolate through the perforated metal panels to irrigate the "forest" of trees growing in the soil. Aside from the physical properties this approach lends the site, the flat ground plane is both an homage to the inherent flatness in the art Walker admires and an honest construction that doesn't just appear to be flat, a fact underscored by revealing the earth room on the facade. The repetitive allover pattern of the paving, the cubic benches-cum–light boxes, and the nonhierarchical grid of trees are all conducive to a visually calm space. The reticent architectural elements serve as a kind of frame for the trees, focusing our attention on their individuality as they change and grow from season to season, bringing life to this otherwise ordered, controlled landscape.

Whereas Walker and Sasaki's design for Keyaki Plaza can be read as an extension of the architecture's formal qualities and as a quiet space for people living in a postindustrial environment, Tom Leader turns up the volume in his Shanghai Carpet, the sunken plaza he is designing for Skidmore, Owings & Merrill's new high-tech development in Shanghai Yang Pu University City Hub (pp. 64–69). Like a vibrantly patterned Persian carpet that sets off a living room, the plaza's richly textured amalgam of paving materials and plants associated with old Shanghai contrasts sharply with the development's rational, modernist architecture. Situated atop a parking garage and at the nexus of multiple transportation routes, Shanghai Carpet lends the hub a distinctive identity. Working in close collaboration with architect Michael Duncan, Leader was inspired by the various materials and patterns found in the streets and sidewalks of old Shanghai, a physical presence that is rapidly vanishing in the expanding city (fig. 7). Without succumbing to nostalgia, Leader, like a *bricoleur*, has expanded the idea of this linear experience into a lively, abstract composition from the odds and ends at hand, embellished with mosses, ferns, and bamboo. The found-object quality of the materials reinforces the notion that the plaza, which is sunken below street level, has been excavated from the city's past. However, with a nod to the high-tech activities in the plaza's surrounding buildings, and reminiscent of the work of artist Jenny Holzer, an LED signboard cuts across the surface of the carpet, providing an unconventional venue for bringing the work of poets and media artists into the garden.[15]

For some sites, the creation of community space is a way to mend a history of conflict or discord. In Beirut a sixteen-year civil war, which ended in 1991, ravaged the city's center, leaving an uninhabited, bombed-out zone separating the Christian east and Muslim

FIG. 8: BEIRUT CITY CENTER, 1991. PHOTOGRAPH BY
GABRIELE BASILICO

west (fig. 8). Since the early 1990s the city has been planning, rebuilding, and restoring on a vast scale, but the idea for a public garden to play a role in healing the fractured city came not from the government or a developer but from an individual. Alexandra Asseily is a psychologist with a keen interest and belief in the idea of forgiveness as a means of assuaging conflict. Hadiqat As-Samah (Garden of Forgiveness), with flowering plants and trees representative of Lebanon's different regions, is intended as a physical manifestation of that idea (pp. 74–79).[16] The mandate given to landscape architects Kathryn Gustafson and Neil Porter describes the ambitious objectives: the garden should be designed to assist the process of postwar reconciliation and healing in Lebanon; create in the heart of the capital a pluralistic social arena that belongs to all; respect the valuable archaeological heritage of the city's five-thousand-year history, with its cycles of preeminence, destruction, and rebirth; and contribute to a new sense of common heritage, identity, and spirit of the future for all Lebanese communities.[17] Recent archaeological excavations mean the garden will be sunken below street level, allowing visitors to physically experience the descent into a serene, secluded, and meditative place that exposes the past. As a transcendent space, Hadiqat As-Samah transports one from the surrounding commercial district to a place integrated with ruins and in touch with natural beauty.

Berlin is another city that has sustained considerable historical trauma in the twentieth century. Unsurprisingly, this has impacted how it is building for the future. As Andreas Huyssen has analyzed so beautifully in his studies such as *Present Pasts: Urban Palimpsests and the Politics of Memory*, the psychological and physical traces of this history are embodied in many of the city's monuments and spaces.[18] After Berlin's reunification, one of the first public spaces to be reconstructed was Invalidenpark, an eighteenth-century park and war memorial that had been paved over as a

parking lot for the East German police (pp. 70–73).[19] In designing the new park, Christophe Girot confronted the problem of how much of the past to reveal, such as the foundations of a late-nineteenth-century chapel or memory of the nearby Berlin Wall. Girot's design reflects the city's desire to move on without forgetting the past. His subtle shaping of the ground plane serves this purpose. In a city devoid of hills and contours, Girot designed a grade change of one percent across the entire two-hundred-meter site so that pedestrians must enter down a broad flight of steps from street level. A low stone frame that circumscribes the park remains level with the surrounding streets, further registering the tilt of the ground plane. Girot has explained that "both psychologically and physiologically the level difference is significant. It marks a new reference plane, a dent in the landscape where something has happened."[20] More recent history is symbolized by the monumental wedge titled *Sinking Wall*, a sculpture that serves as the focal point of the park. Located on the site of the former chapel and Franco-Prussian War memorial whose traces are just barely revealed, the design seems to indicate that the past is perhaps as dangerous to commemorate as to forget. Although Hadiqat As-Samah and Invalidenpark differ in specific intentions and means, both are laden with significance; visitors must recognize and yet transcend the echo of these associations. Such public gathering places—whether designed as stages for the spectacle of modern life or as quiet sites for reflection—draw on historical traces, local associations, and even indigenous plants and materials to give form and content to the contemporary urban landscape.

SIMULATIONS OF NATURE

Ken Smith's roof garden for The Museum of Modern Art (pp. 80–83), with its provocative and ironic camouflage motif, is a fitting metaphor for several traditional aspects of landscape design: simulation of the natural environment and the role of landscape as ground cover and concealment. Smith's design is intended as a decorative landscape to be viewed from above. In

FIG. 7: PHOTO-COLLAGE OF SIDEWALKS AND
STREETS, SHANGHAI, 2004

FIG. 9: ROBERTO BURLE MARX. MINISTRY OF EDUCATION ROOF GARDEN, RIO DE JANEIRO, 1938

FIG. 10: ANDY WARHOL. UNTITLED FROM CAMOUFLAGE. 1987. SCREEN PRINT, 38 x 38" (96.5 x 96.5 CM). THE MUSEUM OF MODERN ART, NEW YORK. JOHN B. TURNER FUND, 2000

this respect, Smith's camouflage motif references an iconic modern roof garden: Roberto Burle Marx's idiosyncratic design for the top of the Ministry of Education in Rio de Janeiro, a building designed by Le Corbusier's disciples Lucio Costa and Oscar Niemeyer in 1936–42 (fig. 9). When seen from above, Burle Marx intended his garden to appear like an abstract painting, belying its spatial and volumetric qualities so apparent when walking among the raised beds. Both Burle Marx's and Smith's gardens juxtapose rational architecture and the curving, organic forms traditionally associated with nature. Smith's design also riffs on the popularity of camouflage in contemporary urban youth culture and on specific works of art in the Museum's collection, namely Andy Warhol's Camouflage series (fig. 10). Composed of plastic plants and boulders, recycled rubber, stone, and glass, Smith's garden suggests other interpretations as well. Not only is it a simulation of real plants and rocks but it is also a subversion of camouflage's function to hide or conceal. Far from camouflaging the institution, the garden trumpets the Museum's location to all those who gaze down upon it. Smith also intended his project as a critique of landscape's complicit role in covering over and hiding abused landscapes, such as sanitary landfills, and formerly industrial sites, such as mines, and in less noxious instances of simply "shrubbing up" a building site. Julie Bargmann, a landscape architect known for her work on polluted sites, refers to this humorously as "putting lipstick on a pig," recalling the deceit inherent even in Repton's landscape transformations. Smith's synthetic roof garden also draws attention to the artifice of constructed landscapes that simulate and evoke nature in its various forms, a practice epitomized by the work of Repton's predecessor, Lancelot "Capability" Brown (1716–1783). By moving and reshaping the ground plane, Brown selectively corrected eyesores, whether natural or man-made, to create naturalistic landscapes that conformed to his aesthetic ideal without revealing the signs of his handiwork.

Catherine Mosbach's new botanical garden in Bordeaux simulates nature but with little intent to

deceive (pp. 84–89). Situated on a long, narrow site in the city's industrial zone beside the Garonne River, the garden demonstrates three landscape types, corresponding to the philosophical idea of the "three natures."[21] The idea, drawn from historical treatises, including those of the ancient Roman writer Cicero (106–43 BC), proposes that the first nature is a landscape unaltered by man—what we might call wilderness. The second nature refers to an agricultural or other utilitarian landscape, including urban infrastructure. The third nature is an artistic or aesthetic landscape. For Bordeaux, Mosbach's environmental garden represents untamed nature—the first nature—which she portrays in constructed simulations.[22] Eleven models correspond to the region's various environments, from the coast to the mountains, thereby replicating the changing ground condition, topography, and plant life. The design intentionally reveals its artifice—these prototypical landscapes are placed on, not in, the ground as though they had each been excavated from their natural habitats and transported to the urban site where they were arranged like a collection of specimens. Their irregular shapes and contours contrast markedly with the fields of crops, which represent the second nature. The diminutive fields are arranged in a group of rectangular beds where the crops are planted in linear, furrowed rows. The third nature, the aestheticized landscape, is represented by Mosbach's water garden. Its studied geometric counterpoint between the paved labyrinth and the flat, glassy surface of the pools evokes a minimalist composition whose serenity is enlivened by the subtle variations in the grid.

Like Mosbach's botanical garden, Kathryn Gustafson's Lurie Garden in downtown Chicago (pp. 96–101) references an indigenous landscape—in this case, the Midwest prairie.[23] But unlike Mosbach, Gustafson had to work with a ground plane that was built on a slab covering an underground parking garage, meaning there was limited soil depth available for plantings. The gentle contours of the beds project up from the supporting structure so that as visitors walk along the paths of the raised prairie gardens at knee and waist height they are immersed in fields of colorful native perennials, selected by plantsman Piet Oudolf. The garden reflects Gustafson's dual interests in sculptural form and color and her artistic training. Her intuitive approach to shaping ground is demonstrated by her working process. She favors white plaster models, devoid of all color, that she molds and carves by hand in the studio. All detail is eliminated except for the contours of the landscape, which she studies in raking light, examining the effect of volume and void, light and shadow. Gustafson studied landscape design in Paris, and it is not surprising that she credits the work of Jacques Sgard as a chief inspiration. Sgard's method is also that of a sculptor giving shape to the earth—whether in a small urban park or the vast scale of a highway interchange.[24] In much of her earlier work, such as the celebrated design for the Shell Headquarters in suburban Paris (pp. 90–95), Gustafson sculpts the ground plane not so much as a simulation of nature but to metaphorically evoke hills and mountains by the ebbs and swells of green grass whose practical function is to conceal an underground parking garage from the residential neighborhood.[25] In Chicago, the prairie garden, with its mix of two hundred species of flowers and grasses, creates a dramatic play of colors and seasonal change. Gustafson's approach to color, exemplified by her impressionistic drawings of Lurie Garden, recalls the painterly approach, although less rigorously, of Gertrude Jekyll (1843–1932), the English garden designer. After studying painting and color, Jekyll turned to garden design, where she applied her ideas about color by juxtaposing flowers of many colors rather than arranging them in isolated groups, seen for example in her own garden at Munstead Wood. The prairie garden in Chicago has similar impressionistic qualities, but which Gustafson constructs as a simulated topography in the urban infrastructure.

Rather than seeing a discrete separation between surface landscape and architectural support, some designers have begun to explore forms and ideas that meld the organic and the built. Foreign Office Architects (FOA), for example, pursued a seamless plasticity of structure, surface, and space in their Yokohama Ferry Terminal (1995–2002) that, despite its informal appearance, is in fact based on rational and complex determinations.[26] The terminal's fluid, multidirectional spaces were intended to read as an extension of the urban ground but also as the result of consistency in the process of construction and material organization. More recently, FOA's investigations have resulted in a new, artificially generated topography for Barcelona's Southeast Coastal Park (pp. 102–09), built entirely on landfill. The park's organic design, with its curved, fluid contours, was inspired by the architects' study of coastal sand dunes as well as the various amenities at the site, which range from outdoor auditoria to places for skateboarding. Alejandro Zaera-Polo has described FOA's design strategy as being a way to "permit organizationally complex landscapes to emerge through the production of topographies artificially generated by a mediated integration of rigorously modeled orders."[27] Such an approach applies to work of many scales and types, whether a park, parking garage, or urban plan. Zaera-Polo has suggested: "The opposition between the rational and the organic that structures the history of landscape design has characterized the history of several disciplines, from philosophy to urbanism.... It is in the overcoming of this opposition that we think the possibility of an emerging landscape—and city and architecture—may exist. The emerging landscape will be characterized by developments already occurring in biotechnology, artificial intelligence, design and lifestyle, where the natural and the artificial have become virtually indistinguishable."[28] This exploration of connectivity and flow leads to complex forms that blur the distinctions between landscape, infrastructure, and architecture.

The work of Enric Miralles and Carme Pinós at Igualada Cemetery Park in Igualada, Spain (pp. 110–15), examines a different issue of transforming the ground plane of an existing site through the integration of architecture and landscape.[29] Their task was to reshape the terrain of an arid river valley, which has the appearance of an abandoned quarry and whose poor-quality soil

FIG. 11: DENNY REGRADE, SEATTLE, C. 1909

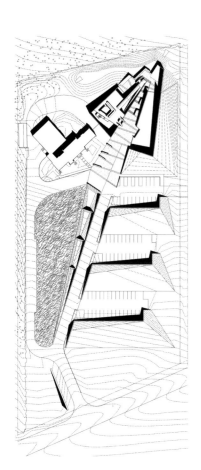

FIG. 12: WEISS/MANFREDI ARCHITECTS.
MUSEUM OF THE EARTH, ITHACA, NEW YORK,
2000–03. SITE PLAN

offered little practical use, into a cemetery.[30] The architects excavated a wide path and framed it with sloping walls housing crypts built into the landscape. Like Hadiqat As-Samah in Beirut, the gentle descent into the valley effectively removes one from ordinary routines by shutting out distractions from the surroundings. The path, framed by the crypts, and the park's wild landscape make for a psychologically rich experience that puts the visitor in close physical contact with the earth. The paving stones from the site, embedded with railroad ties of a near-human scale laid in a random pattern, reinforce this perception. In accepting the reality of this seemingly unremarkable site and transforming it with humble materials, the architects created a congruence and continuity between the excavated space, the constructed ground and walls, and the surrounding natural landscape that is intended to evoke memory, loss, and serenity.

Where Miralles and Pinós created a new topography for the Igualada site through excavation, Weiss/Manfredi Architects is constructing landforms where none previously existed for the Seattle Art Museum's Olympic Sculpture Park in downtown Seattle (pp. 116–23).[31] The fragmented site, bisected by a railroad and a four-lane road, lacked coherence and unity. Following the removal of contaminated ground from this former oil transfer station, the site required landfill. Weiss/Manfredi's project is not the first time this waterfront neighborhood has been remade. The most dramatic of several previous interventions, known as Denny Regrade, took place nearly a century ago when a developer deliberately eroded the bluff by hosing down the earth in order to render the site more level and therefore more attractive to development (fig. 11). A principal problem faced by Weiss/Manfredi was how to connect the three separate parcels divided by the transportation routes and simultaneously construct a new topography with clean landfill. One solution might have been to conceal the ruptures completely, a strategy other designers have used effectively to hide sunken highways, notably Michel Corajoud's landscaped deck that covers the

massive cleavage wrought by the A-1 in Paris. Instead, Weiss/Manfredi designed landforms that partially cover Elliott Avenue and the Burlington Northern Santa Fe Railroad tracks so that a continuous pedestrian path zigzags across the sloping site, largely determining the park's new contours. Rather than eliminate the train and car, the design makes the urban infrastructure and the speed of modern life no less a part of the site's urban reality than the pedestrians with their view of the scenic harbor. Moreover, the architects and the museum's curators are considering the highway's embankments as possible venues for art projects.

This reshaping of the ground inspired Weiss/Manfredi to analyze the complex relationships of seemingly contradictory functions—between the new and existing infrastructures, the landscapes of the Northwest that will contribute to the park's form and character, the urban context, and its program as a gallery for outdoor sculpture. The intersection of landscape and the built environment characterizes much of Weiss/Manfredi's work. Their design for the Museum of the Earth in Ithaca, New York, explores the relationship between architecture and topography in several respects, including a series of tilted landforms that function as water-retention devices in the parking area (fig. 12). The sculpted berms descend across the sloping site and echo the Finger Lakes region's natural geological formations created by glaciers. A path seems to cleave the museum apart as if a massive wedge had gouged the site, altering the topography in its wake. At Ithaca and in the new topography designed for the Olympic Sculpture Park, Weiss/Manfredi's integration of art, ecology, and program defines their strategy for constructing new sites.

These new artificially constructed environments, whether an urban rooftop or part of a regional redevelopment, simulate many aspects of natural landscapes. They are not intended to deceive the viewer, however, nor conform to any one idealized form of nature. By means of imitation, excavation, and the inte-

FIG. 13: RICHARD HAAG ASSOCIATES. GAS WORKS PARK, SEATTLE, 1971–75

gration of architecture and infrastructure, architects and landscape architects construct new topographies and accommodate new programs.

THE BAD AND THE BEAUTIFUL

Defunct steel mills, sanitary landfills, polluted riverfronts once dedicated to commerce and industry—these so-called brownfields are among the abused sites that have become our new parks. Their former uses exhausted, architects, landscape architects, and urban planners are asked to envision their postindustrial transformation into places for leisure activities and redevelopment. Traditionally, industry and urban infrastructures pose a threat to our notion of landscape, at least one based on a pastoral ideal. The nature exemplified by eighteenth- and nineteenth-century landscapes and in paintings of the period offered an alternative to the constraints of organized society, seen for example in the relationship between New York City's Central Park and the urban fabric surrounding it. While those bucolic ideals reflect the values and landscape of a preindustrial, largely agrarian world, today the designer's task is to transform what we might think of as blighted sites into places that challenge not only our preconception of what makes a park but also what makes a landscape beautiful. This shift in attitude was prefigured in the artwork and writings of American artist Robert Smithson, whose 1967 essay "A Tour of the Monuments of Passaic, New Jersey" called attention to the fact that this kind of pervasive and fantastic—if not ugly—man-made landscape held the clues to our future.[32] Smithson's work was prophetic and influenced the way some designers, Peter Latz and George Hargreaves among them, look at the relationship between the industrial landscape and nature, between the ugly and beautiful.

The adaptation of industrial ruins in a contemporary park has an important precedent in Richard Haag Associates' Gas Works Park in Seattle (1971–75).[33] The gas plant on a nearly twenty-acre site on Lake Union had shut down in 1956. The industrial structures were scheduled to be removed but Richard Haag, seeing them as works of abstract art not unlike the mysterious,

mechanical sculptures of Jean Tinguely, decided to keep them (fig. 13). The designer met with community resistance in the process. Haag described his personal evolution of seeing the industrial past in a new light: "I began with the site. I haunted the buildings and let the spirit of the place enjoin mine. I began seeing what I liked and then I liked what I saw—new eyes for old. Permanent oil slicks became plains with outcroppings of concrete, industrial middens were drumlins, the towers were ferro-forests and their brooding presence became the most sacred of symbols. I accepted these gifts, and decided to absolve the community's vindictive feeling towards the gas plant. This vanishing species of the industrial revolution was saved from extinction through adaptive use."[34]

When Peter Latz designed Duisburg-Nord Landscape Park (pp. 124–31) on the grounds of the former Thyssen Steelworks in western Germany, one of the most significant new parks of the last decade, like Haag he believed the opposition of the natural and the industrial was not a realistic model.[35] The site's industrial ruins—including towering smokestacks, cavernous ore bunkers, and bermed railroad tracks—constituted not only a significant part of the region's history but were in themselves fantastic structures. Latz resisted the impulse to eliminate the industrial traces of the nearly six-hundred-acre site, believing that if the realms of nature and industry were combined the experience would be richer. His scheme raised the ire of many landscape architects who believed that parks should conform to more conventional designs and conservationists who had other ideas about remediating a toxic area. The need to clean the polluted site meant designing new systems for water. The ground had varying levels of toxicity and pH levels suited to different kinds of vegetation. Some areas were capped, hopelessly polluted soil was removed, and the remaining areas, if left alone, will be naturally remediated over time by pioneer species such as birch and poplar. Latz realized that a designer cannot control such a large and complex site, and that natural processes will to some extent determine the qualities of the changing landscape.

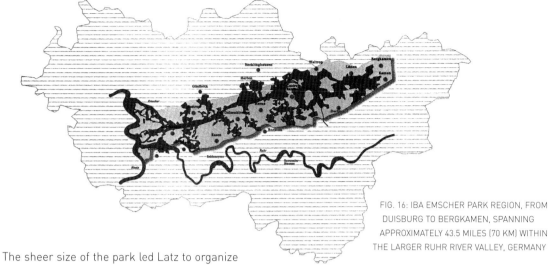

FIG. 16: IBA EMSCHER PARK REGION, FROM DUISBURG TO BERGKAMEN, SPANNING APPROXIMATELY 43.5 MILES (70 KM) WITHIN THE LARGER RUHR RIVER VALLEY, GERMANY

FIG. 14: PETER LATZ. DUISBURG-NORD LANDSCAPE PARK, DUISBURG, GERMANY, 1990–2002

FIG. 15: WILLIAM AISLABIE. FOUNTAINS ABBEY, RIVER SKELL, NORTH YORKSHIRE, ENGLAND. 1768

The sheer size of the park led Latz to organize the land in terms of zones based on activities, systems of plants and water, even layers of paths, such as the elevated catwalks, belvederes, and the land art–like berms of the former railroad tracks that fan out across the site. The industrial ruins, which could easily have been subjects for Bernd and Hilla Becher, who aestheticized German industrial culture in their photographs, have transcended their original rational function. While some have been adapted for various leisure activities, the awesome structures evoke associations, emotions, and an aura of mystery that inspired Latz to construct narratives and stories that alluded to a mythic past (fig. 14). The designer has cited as an inspiration Bomarzo, the sixteenth-century Italian Renaissance garden with fantastic sculptures carved from giant boulders of tufa that allude to humanistic themes inspired by great literary works such as Dante's *Inferno* and Virgil's *Aeneid*.[36] Latz finds the ruins of Duisburg-Nord equally fantastic. His appreciation of the industrial infrastructure also recalls the cult of ruins that was so fashionable in the great landscape parks of the eighteenth century, such as at Fountains Abbey, designed by William Aislabie, where the medieval ruins of a Cistercian abbey are approached from a distance along a waterway threading through a meadow (fig. 15).[37] At Duisburg-Nord, Latz has reintroduced allegory and a sense of the sublime into contemporary landscape. We can perceive these relics in awe—metaphorically as mountains, as Latz himself has suggested, or perhaps more ominously as reminders of the human and natural destruction wrought by the twentieth-century ferro-industrial complex so closely identified with the Emscher region. The traces of the past define not only the park and the region's culture, but also determine the park's future as much by the myriad recreational and cultural programs taking place at Duisburg-Nord as by the diverse native and exotic plants that are colonizing the site and beginning a process of natural succession. There is a certain irony to be found in a site that once existed solely to function

with the efficiency of industry now being turned over to the unpredictability of natural processes and unforeseen human activities.

Duisburg-Nord Landscape Park was the showcase of the IBA (Internationale Bauausstellung, or International Building Exhibition), which under the direction of Karl Ganser sponsored approximately one hundred art, landscape, and development projects from 1989 to 1999. These projects were intended to environmentally, economically, socially, and aesthetically revitalize the Emscher region, which covers an area of 115 square miles, including several large regional parks, forging a connection between Dortmund and the Rhine (fig. 16). The formerly industrial region has been substantially reshaped by the excavating and piling of mountains of earth, coal, and slag heaps—a legacy that will take decades to grapple with. Some projects, like Duisburg-Nord, are permanent; others were ephemeral, such as Martha Schwartz and Markus Jatsch's *Power Lines*, an outdoor artwork that called attention to industrial and political power (fig. 17). Schwartz chose a site under towering electrical power lines where she planted a series of cornfields to form parallel rows of "dashes." A second line of hay bales, wrapped in fiery-red plastic, intersected the power lines and was aligned with a statue of Bismarck on a nearby hill. At their intersection, a black room, formed by hay bales wrapped in black plastic with a floor of coal, symbolized the ominous power that can wreak such environmental and human destruction, a reminder that the northern Ruhr Valley had been the country's preeminent industrial district. Germany's rustbelt is also identified as one of the world's "mega cities," with a regional population approaching six million people. Thomas Sieverts, an architect and urban planner, has characterized the region as a particularly troubling example of intermediate urban sprawl with few historic centers or identifiable cores—a region that doesn't conform to our ideals of either city or land-

FIG. 18: HARGREAVES ASSOCIATES. BYXBEE PARK, PALO ALTO, CALIFORNIA, 1990

FIG. 17: MARTHA SCHWARTZ, INC. *POWER LINES*, GELSENKIRCHEN, GERMANY, 1999, IBA EMSCHER PARK

scape.[38] Rather than seek old models, the Emscher projects, including Duisburg-Nord, exemplify a positive new perception of the industrial landscape that is compatible with leisure and cultural activities and conservation of the environment.

The remaking and reinterpretation of Duisburg-Nord was based largely on the traces left by historical intervention. For the Parc de la Cour du Maroc in Paris (pp. 138–43), which will occupy a former rail yard, the memory of the site's utilitarian past similarly inspired the designers, Michel and Claire Corajoud and Georges Descombes. Although the tracks have been removed, the long narrow site informed the project's general concept. The rational alignment of the long parallel rows of tracks is adapted here as an ordering device that arranges the various park activities and types of gardens into discrete zones. The designers have planned a gravel garden that explicitly recalls the ballast that once covered the ground. Intrigued by the pioneer plants that have already taken root in the abandoned site's inhospitable environment, the Corajouds and Descombes intend this rough ground to appeal as much to the botanist for the varieties of plants specified for the gravel garden as to kids who might be drawn to such an informal environment for recreation. As at Duisburg-Nord, the new park bears traces of the rational system that gave order to the previously utilitarian landscape.

In addition to grappling with the legacy of industrial advances—and a century's worth of residue and detritus—designers are often asked to transform sanitary landfills and other kinds of waste-treatment centers into parks. This is not an entirely new phenomenon. In the 1860s J. C. Alphand transformed a strange crescent-shaped site in Paris that had been quarried and subsequently served as a sewage dump and even a mass grave into a public park—the Parc des Buttes-Chaumont. The site's conversion to a park challenged conventional ideas regarding beauty and the relationship between nature and culture.[39] As in Paris, many industrial cities in the late nineteenth century began to dispose of their trash on their peripheries, burying it under

streets, dumping it in old quarries, or, when they could, simply tossing garbage into the sea. Low-lying swampy areas, which we now call wetlands, were singled out for landfills because they were thought to have no other usable, redeeming, or profitable features. At the time there was little awareness of the vital ecological role of wetlands, including filtering pollutants from water, nor did these mosquito breeding grounds conform to our idea of a beautiful landscape.[40]

Such was the situation Hargreaves Associates faced at Crissy Field, the former military airstrip on San Francisco Bay, which among other things involved the restoration of a tidal marsh (pp. 132–37). The army had systematically eliminated the wetlands over several decades by using it as a dumping ground and landfill to create a solid, level surface for a staging ground, firing range, and other activities.[41] George Hargreaves was well suited to tackle this project, having transformed several landfills and wetlands into parks using different strategies. To create Byxbee Park in Palo Alto, California, a thirty-acre retired landfill was treated as a large earthwork that concealed sixty-foot-high mounds of trash (fig. 18). The program was essentially to beautify the site and plant the ground. Hargreaves sculpted the ground to form berms and contours and, working with artists Michael Oppenheimer and Peter Richards, designed an art installation with found objects such as telephone poles and highway barriers. The ground was planted with native species that would thrive with minimal care. The strategy was predicated on Hargreaves's keen interest in natural processes, which assume control of a site after he establishes the ordering structure. Hargreaves has described this approach as a radical departure from conventional design, where a desired result is to be strictly maintained: "I'm setting up a framework on the land. Then vegetation, people, and water wash over it. This is completely different from what I was brought up to do. It's a cousin of [Richard Serra's] lead pours: you set up the process, but you don't control the end product."[42] Hargreaves's focus on process is reflected in most

FIG. 20: ABALOS & HERREROS. VALDEMINGÓMEZ CITY DUMP
AND RECYCLING PLANT, MADRID, 1999

FIG. 19: HARGREAVES ASSOCIATES. SYDNEY
OLYMPICS, VIEW OF SCULPTED LANDFORMS
AND MAN-MADE WETLANDS AT HOMEBUSH
BAY, 2000

of his large public works, notably at the 2000 Sydney Olympics, where a brickworks, slaughterhouse, and munitions dump occupied a wetlands and forest for decades before its recent transformation into an environmental "showpiece" and public space for the international sports event (fig. 19).[43]

The transformation of Crissy Field reflects the need to serve a number of public interests, including the preservation of the historic grass runway, wetlands and dune restoration, and the provision of recreational spaces. Hargreaves decided to restore the wetlands by removing tons of earth and artificial fill (much of which was reused to create the airstrip's new topography) and reopen a channel between the new wetlands and San Francisco Bay. The site also held traces of a pre-military past. Archaeological remains of the Muwekma Ohlone Indian Tribe were buried there. Appropriately, on November 9, 1999, when the mouth to the bay was reopened, setting in motion the process of restoring the wetlands' natural ecological processes, Native Americans participated in the ceremony. Hargreaves's design for the restored tidal marsh is intended to look like a natural environment, giving the site a truly Reptonian makeover. Without the juxtaposition of the before-and-after pictures one would have little idea of the extensive intervention. The landscape architect's transformation of other parts of Crissy Field—the shoreline, dunes, recreation areas, and historic airstrip—was no less dramatic.

If one solution is to conceal mounds of trash under new vegetation, such as at Byxbee Park, and another is to remove landfill from a site as Hargreaves did at Crissy Field, a third alternative is to bring the trash into the foreground of the public's experience. The Spanish architects Iñaki Abalos and Juan Herreros have designed several projects that reveal this reality of consumer culture in an effort to promote waste reduction, recycling, and safeguards of the environment. At their Valdemingómez recycling plant in Madrid they made a public showcase of the inner workings of the high-tech recycling center with its multitiered green roof. The center is located beside a former dump, which will eventually become a regional park (fig. 20). Even more visible

to the public is their recent Northeast Coastal Park in Barcelona (pp. 144–47) that combines a recycling center and former incinerator with a new public park constructed on artificial landfill on the shore of the Mediterranean Sea. Abalos and Herreros have described this paradoxical coupling as an effort "to create one of Barcelona's most extensive natural public spaces."[44]

As part of a larger international trend, Northeast Coastal Park exemplifies a new kind of park that no longer hides trash from public view.[45] By making waste treatment visible to the public, the hope is that people will become more educated about and sensitive to the impact they inflict on the urban infrastructure and environment with the tons of trash they generate. The demonstration waste facility coupled with an alluring new public amenity—the coastal park—reveals, rather than conceals, a previously hidden reality of urban life. The new public space begins with an esplanade studded with clusters of palm trees that culminates in a vast colorful mosaic by artist Albert Oehlen depicting swimming fish. The mosaic-covered ground is part of a centuries-long Spanish and Portuguese tradition. Before designing Northeast Coastal Park, Abalos and Herreros and Oehlen had previously collaborated on urban design projects in Rio de Janeiro in which mosaic ornament created an identity much as it does in Barcelona. Their work in Rio was undoubtedly inspired by the Brazilian city's extensive landfill projects along the coast that were enhanced by Burle Marx's mosaic paving, notably his wavelike, serpentine patterns of colored tiles lining Copacabana Beach (1970). In Barcelona, the Northeast Coastal Park is part of much larger urban intervention— the UNESCO-organized Forum 2004, which includes the Southeast Coastal Park (see pp. 102–09) and projects by Herzog & de Meuron, Elias Torres, Beth Gali, and others—that combines cultural and environmental programs. The overall project significantly expands the public open space in Barcelona. It is a testament to the city's political will and leadership under Josep Acebillo, chief architect of the city council of Barcelona, who has continued the extensive improvements to the city's

public landscape begun over a decade ago in conjunction with the 1992 Olympics that began the recent construction of Barcelona's waterfront.

Field Operations' design for the Fresh Kills *lifescape* (pp. 156–61) on New York City's Staten Island, although exponentially larger than Byxbee Park, Crissy Field, and Northeast Coastal Park, parallels these sites in several of its objectives: to conceal mounds of trash that have been capped and planted over, restore wetlands, and transform a landfill into a recreational park.[46] When Robert Moses established the Fresh Kills landfill in 1948 it was considered a model waste facility: tidal wetlands would be transformed from breeding grounds for mosquitoes into useful land suited to the residential communities, parkland, and industrial zone he envisioned. Moses anticipated the landfill to be active for three years, but Fresh Kills did not close until March 2001, serving a city that produces more garbage than any other in the world for over half a century. New York City's Department of Sanitation is the world's largest, and today collects more than 12,000 tons of refuse daily from residences and institutions, while businesses generate another 13,000 tons of refuse daily. Having reached its maximum capacity for fill and with a concern for the environment and for the residents of Staten Island, the inevitable question was what to do with more than fifty years' worth of garbage. The most conspicuous legacy is the two mountains of refuse. Their noxious contents concealed under a protective membrane that cannot be broken, there is little opportunity to reshape the contours of the ground. Rather, the contained garbage is camouflaged under a thin layer of soil planted with strip crops that create a green surface. The size of Fresh Kills' mountains recalls the residue of other colossal man-made interventions, such as mine tailings, that are similarly inhospitable to ecological remediation. The magnitude of these desolate sites is impressive, yet the possibility for their transformation seems limited to becoming giant entropic earthworks. In reshaping the MacLeod Gold Mine tailings in Geraldton, Canada, Martha Schwartz created a roadside tourist attraction

in order to draw visitors to the economically challenged community (fig. 21).[47] She sculpted the hills into distinctly man-made landforms that were visually compelling, covered them with topsoil, and planted native grasses. Faced with a somewhat similar situation, Shlomo Aronson confronted the massive phosphate mines in the Negev Desert in Israel. In this hostile environment with poor soil, the landscape architect designed a monumental earthwork by moving and reshaping millions of tons of earth (fig. 22).[48] But unlike these mining projects, the mountains of garbage at Fresh Kills cannot be penetrated or reshaped except by the vicissitudes of time and decomposition.

The complexity of the Fresh Kills site required many kinds of responses, from the engineering and technical skills needed to manage the leachate (contaminated liquid resulting from water passing through the mounds of garbage) and off-gassing from the slowly decomposing mounds to the kinds of public programs and recreational activities envisioned in Field Operations' colorful renderings. James Corner calls his master plan *lifescape*, a reminder that the site is a living, changing environment. Corner ensures that his designs retain a certain fluidity, believing that "a good strategy is a highly organized plan (spatial, programmatic, or logistical) that is at the same time flexible and structurally capable of significant adaptation in response to changing circumstances."[49]

Such an approach predicated on time and change—two phenomena inherent in landscape and its processes—is also characteristic of Michel Desvigne's transformations for large industrial urban sectors, such as London's three-hundred-acre Greenwich Peninsula on the Thames River (pp. 148–51) and a five-mile stretch along the Garonne River on Bordeaux's right bank (pp. 152–55). The idea behind his designs for Greenwich Peninsula and Bordeaux is to give the land the texture of an earlier, untamed state. By planting thousands of trees and shrubs, which will be thinned as they grow, the landscape will evolve over many years in a manner

FIG. 23: MICHEL DESVIGNE, DESVIGNE & DALNOKY. GREENWICH PENINSULA, LONDON, 1997–2000. VIEW OF PARK IN 2004

FIG. 24: MICHEL DESVIGNE AND CHRISTINE DALNOKY, DESVIGNE & DALNOKY. RUE DE MEAUX, COURTYARD GARDEN, PARIS, 1990

that approximates natural growth and succession (fig. 23). The goal is not to simply return land to an unadulterated state, but to restore it to the point that it is possible to develop—what Desvigne calls an "intermediate landscape." These projects might be described as first drafts in histories that will unfold over the next half century. The groves of trees and plants he envisions are intended to be adaptable and resilient to unpredictable demands as the surrounding areas continue to change in decades to come. To design anything more specific on these large sites, Desvigne argues, would be premature in the absence of a firm program, an approach that has been described as a kind of calculated detachment.[50] As a small-scale example of the overall effect he wants to establish on these abused landscapes, Desvigne points to the birch forest he and Christine Dalnoky designed for the courtyard of Renzo Piano's Rue de Meaux apartment building in Paris (fig. 24). Here they planted a dense grove of birches and understory plants in a manner that suggests the apartment building had been constructed around a piece of preexisting forest.[51]

　　Desvigne's projects also draw inspiration from Frederick Law Olmsted, America's great nineteenth-century landscape architect, who once explained to his son: "I have all my life been considering distant effects and always sacrificing immediate success and applause to that of the future. In laying out Central Park we determined to think of no result to be realized in less than forty years."[52] In particular, Desvigne cites Olmsted's famous Emerald Necklace—a string of six parks threading through Boston and Brookline, Massachusetts—as one of the great examples of a constructed landscape in the urban environment (fig. 25). From 1878 to 1896 Olmsted transformed one thousand acres stretching five miles into a green buffer that continues to enhance Boston's urban environment. Desvigne is similarly inspired by aerial views of large tracts of land—whether wilderness or tree farms—that illustrate the figure-

ground relationship between trees and open space utterly lacking on a site such as the Greenwich Peninsula after it was scraped clear of toxic ground. At Bordeaux the ambition is much greater: 330 acres will be transformed into green spaces. In time, the geographic center of the city will become a park and the area around it will be redeveloped for residential housing, schools, and commerce. One of the first projects to be constructed in the heart of the district was Mosbach's Bordeaux Botanical Garden, built in conjunction with an earlier master plan. Desvigne's drawings engage the larger region and are intended as anticipations of what Bordeaux might become over time. The specific parks and public spaces have not yet been designed. On an urbanistic level, the plan also seeks a greater balance between the historic left bank and the postindustrial right bank. The city, under the leadership of Mayor Alain Juppé, purchased over one hundred acres—a demonstration of political will on a scale that is rare in Europe and recalls the civic ambitions exercised in Olmsted's era.

EXPANDING THE FIELD

The rapid pace at which cities are remaking themselves on vast tracts of land is changing the discipline of landscape architecture and urban design. The role of open spaces in redefining the modern city has led to the development of the idea of landscape as urbanism. In the mid-1990s James Corner and architect Charles Waldheim coined the term "landscape urbanism" to describe the shift from architecture as the traditional progenitor of city form to landscape as a new paradigm. Corner and Waldheim recognized landscape as a medium that most closely approximates the open-endedness of urbanization. Landscape traditionally concerns the temporal, change, transformation, indeterminacy, and succession. Landscape, like urbanism, is as much about form as process.[53] Adriaan Geuze of West 8, who pursues an expanded field of activity in his work, has explained, "Architects and industrial designers often see their designs as a final prod-

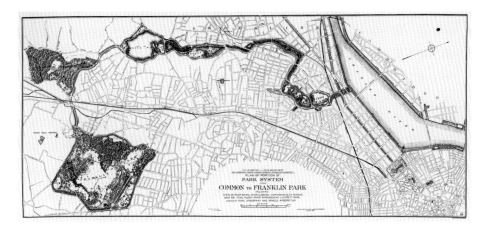

FIG. 25: FREDERICK LAW OLMSTED, OLMSTED & ELIOT, LANDSCAPE ARCHITECTS. PLAN OF THE PARK SYSTEM FROM BOSTON COMMON TO FRANKLIN PARK, JANUARY 1894. LITHOGRAPH

uct of genius, whose aesthetic entirety originated in their minds. A design like that is thrown off by the slightest damage. Landscape architects have learned to put that in perspective, because they know their designs are continually adapted and transformed. We have learned to see landscape not as a *fait accompli*, but as the result of countless forces and initiatives."[54]

Significantly, Waldheim cites the Parc de la Villette competition of 1982, which called for the transformation of a 125-acre site in Paris formerly occupied by slaughterhouses into a twenty-first-century park, as one of the first projects signaling a shift in the field. He suggests that the competition "began a trajectory of postmodern urban park making in which landscape itself was conceived as a complex medium capable of articulating relations among urban infrastructure, public events, and indeterminate urban futures for large post industrial sites."[55] Bernard Tschumi's winning scheme for Parc de la Villette and the entry by Rem Koolhaas's Office for Metropolitan Architecture placed an emphasis on program and indeterminate form because it was unclear how the site might be used over time. In this view, landscape offers a strategy for accommodating and integrating—rather than opposing—urban activities, infrastructure, and architecture, recognizing that sites must adapt and respond to change over time. Ultimately, this has led to a greater understanding of landscape as a model for urbanism: layered, nonhierarchical, flexible, and strategic. More recently Corner has suggested that contemporary urban projects require "a new kind of synthetic imagination—a new form of practice in which architecture, landscape, planning, ecology, engineering, social policy, and political process are both understood *and* coordinated as an interrelated field."[56] This characterizes the approach that Field Operations has adopted for large-scale, long-range projects such as Fresh Kills, their competition entry for Downsview Park, Toronto, in 2000,[57] and in their project to redesign many miles of Philadelphia's

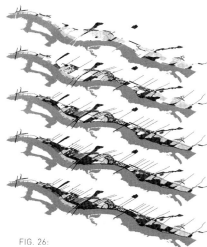

FIG. 26:
FIELD OPERATIONS.
NORTH DELAWARE RIVERFRONT,
PHILADELPHIA, 2001. PHASING OF
REDEVELOPMENT AT FIVE-YEAR INTERVALS

North Delaware Riverfront (fig. 26). An integrative approach drawing upon many disciplines, including architecture, landscape architecture, and infrastructure engineering, characterizes other projects as well—such as Weiss/ Manfredi's Olympic Sculpture Park and Hargreaves Associates' Crissy Field—reflecting the complexities of constructing public spaces in the urban realm.

The open spaces surveyed here illustrate many kinds of ground conditions—artificial surfaces on top of parking garages, large complex landfills and polluted sites, and the ruins of historic cities. Although specific circumstances and programs differ, these designed spaces share an ability to engage the public, their imagination and emotions, to bring them in contact with the outdoors, the seasons, and what we call nature. Not surprisingly the complexity of many of these urban sites blurs traditional boundaries between architecture, infrastructure, and constructed landscapes, demanding a greater coordination between the open spaces of the ground plane and the figuration of elements on the ground. This has always been germane to the design of cities. Architect Iñaki Abalos has suggested his profession needs to overcome the traditional polarization of architecture and landscape architecture. He objects to the dichotomies that typically characterize the two professions: with architects focused on the artificial, solid, and industrial, and landscape architects on the void and nature. Like other architects and landscape architects whose works are shown here, he asks that we recognize a greater role for urban space: "We can only imagine... the landscape-subject as the more complex learning process, calling for an initiatory crossing towards understanding the real monument to be built: contemporary public space."[58] Building these monuments requires civic leadership and creative vision that combines art and ecological processes in responsible, meaningful, and unabashedly beautiful ways.

NOTES

I would like to thank Bryan Fuermann, landscape historian, for his comments and suggestions based on an earlier draft of this essay.

1 See, for example, Julia Czerniak, "Challenging the Pictorial: Recent Landscape Practice," *Assemblage* 34 (December 1997): 110–20, and James Corner, "Representation and Landscape: Drawing and Making in the Landscape Medium," *Word and Image* (July–September 1992): 243–74.

2 Geuze, as quoted by Chris Young, "Culture Vulture," *Landscape Design*, no. 280 (May 1999): 17.

3 Bart Lootsma, "The Tradition of the New: West 8 and the Dutch Landscape," in *Het Landschap* (Antwerp: de Singel, 1995), 103.

4 Adriaan Geuze, "Accelerating Darwin," in Gerrit Smienk, ed., *Nederlandse landschapsarchitectuur, Tussen traditie en experiment* (Amsterdam: THOTH in association with the Academie van Bouwkunst [Amsterdamse Hogeschool voor de Kunsten], 1993), as translated and quoted in Lootsma "The Tradition of the New," 90. In his essay, Lootsma offers further analysis of Geuze's response to the Parc de la Villette competition, particularly the entry by Rem Koolhaas and the Office for Metropolitan Architecture.

5 See Jason Prior, "Piccadilly Gardens, Manchester," *Topos: European Landscape Magazine* 32 (June 2002): 86–91.

6 Martha Schwartz, "Landscape and Common Culture since Modernism," in Marc Treib, ed., *Modern Landscape Architecture: A Critical Review* (Cambridge, Mass., and London: The MIT Press, 1993), 263. In this essay Schwartz traces her interests in modern art and landscape design.

7 Ibid., 264.

8 Little has been published about Alsop's Bradford plan. See Ed Dorrell, "After Barnsley, Alsop Adds Bradford to Its Northern Regeneration," *Architects' Journal* 218 (October 16, 2003): 10. For a somewhat critical review of the project, see Peter Davey, "Outrage," *Architectural Review* 214 (November 2003): 24.

9 For background on Keyaki Plaza, see Yoji Sasaki, *Landscape Design* (Tokyo: Marumo Publishing, 2004); and Peter Walker, *Saitama Plaza: Forest in the Sky* (forthcoming). I am grateful to Peter Walker for sharing an advance copy of this book with me and for explaining the complexities of the project in conversation, June 4, 2004.

10 See Peter Walker, "The Practice of Landscape Architecture in the Postwar United States," in *Modern Landscape Architecture*, ed. Marc Treib, 250–59; and Peter Walker, *Minimalist Gardens* (Washington, D.C., and Cambridge, Mass.: Spacemaker Press, 1997). See esp. Walker's essay "Classicism, Modernism, and Minimalism in the Landscape," 17–23.

11 See Dan Kiley and Jane Amidon, *Dan Kiley: Complete Works* (Boston: Bullfinch, 1999), 106–11.

12 Walker, *Minimalist Gardens*, 17.

13 Ibid., 21.

14 This can also be considered an homage of sorts to Walter de Maria's *Earth Room*, which he first created in 1968 by filling the exhibition space at the Galerie Heiner Friedrich in Munich with fifty cubic meters of earth.

15 The LED strip recalls the glowing line of light at Peter Walker and Partner's IBM Japan Makuhari Building (1991), a project Leader worked on briefly when he was in Walker's office. This project is illustrated in Walker, *Minimalist Gardens*, 142–43.

16 See Neil Porter, "Garden of Forgiveness – Hadiqat As-Samah, Beirut," *Topos: European Landscape Magazine* 45 (December 2003): 57–64.

17 Nasser Chammaa, foreword to "The Garden of Forgiveness in Beirut Central District: An International Landscape Design Competition" (unpublished competition booklet by Solidere, the development company charged with rebuilding central Beirut, August 1999).

18 Andreas Huyssen, *Present Pasts: Urban Palimpsests and the Politics of Memory* (Stanford, Calif.: Stanford University Press, 2003).

19 For more on Invalidenpark, see Lisa Diedrich, "Der Invalidenpark in Berlin (Invaliden Park, Berlin)," *Topos: European Landscape Magazine* 22 (March 1998): 69–74.

20 Christophe Girot, "Berlin Invaliden Park, Some Traces in the Future" (unpublished manuscript).

21 John Dixon Hunt has developed the idea of the three natures based on historical sources. See Hunt, *Greater Perfections: The Practice of Garden Theory* (Philadelphia: University of Pennsylvania Press, 2000), esp. "The Idea of a Garden and the Three Natures," 32–75.

22 For more on the Bordeaux Botanical Garden, see Catherine Mosbach, interview by Michel Menu, "From Nature to Culture," *Pages Paysages*, no. 9 (November 2002): 60–70. This is reprinted in John Dixon Hunt, ed., *Studies in the History of Gardens and Designed Landscapes* 23 (summer 2003): 175–81.

23 For background about the competition and what is now called Lurie Garden, see Charles Waldheim, *Constructed Ground: The Millennium Garden Design Competition* (Urbana and Chicago: University of Illinois Press, 2001).

24 On Sgard's work, see Annette Vigny, *Jacques Sgard: Paysagiste & Urbaniste* (Liege: Mardaga, 1995).

25 For more about Gustafson's work, see Leah Levy, *Kathryn Gustafson: Sculpting the Land* (Washington, D.C., and Cambridge, Mass.: Spacemaker Press, 1998).

26 See Foreign Office Architects, *The Yokohama Project* (Barcelona: Actar, 2002); and Foreign Office Architects, *Phylogenesis: foa's ark* (Barcelona: Actar, 2003).

27 Foreign Office Architects, *Phylogenesis*, 58.

28 Alejandro Zaera-Polo, "On Landscape," in *Landscape Urbanism: A Manual for the Machinic Landscape*, ed. Mohsen Mostafavi and Ciro Najle, (London: Architectural Association, 2003), 132.

29 For more information about the cemetery, see *Enric Miralles, 1983–2000: Mental Maps and Social Landscapes* (Madrid: El Croquis, 2002), esp. 50–77, and the excellent discussion in Anita Berrizbeitia and Linda Pollak, *Inside Outside: Between Architecture and Landscape* (Gloucester, Mass.: Rockport Publishers, 1999), 68–75.

30 Carme Pinós and Benedetta Tagliabue (Miralles's widow and partner) both confirmed that the site had never been a quarry, although several publications about Miralles's work have suggested it was. Conversations with author, May 9, 2004.

31 For general information on this project, see Amanda Reeser, "Olympic Sculpture Park, Weiss/Manfredi Architects," *Praxis* 4 (2002): 66–69.

32 Robert Smithson, in Nancy Holt, ed., *The Writings of Robert Smithson* (New York: New York University Press, 1979), 52–57.

33 For more about Haag's project, see William S. Saunders, ed., *Richard Haag: Bloedel Reserve and Gas Works Park* (New York: Princeton Architectural Press with the Harvard University Graduate School of Design, 1998), in particular Elizabeth K. Meyer, "Seized by Sublime Sentiments," 5–28. Also, "Gas Works Park," in Jory Johnson, *Modern Landscape Architecture* (New York: Abbeville Press, 1991), 199–207.

34 Richard Haag, "It Was Gas," *Outreach*, Ohio State University, Department of Landscape Architecture (spring 1982): n.p.

35 Much has been written about Duisburg-Nord Landscape Park and the IBA Emscher Park project overall. See, for example, the entire issue of *Topos: European Landscape Magazine* 26 (March 1999); and Peter Latz, "Landscape Park Duisburg-Nord: The Metamorphosis of an Industrial Site," in Niall Kirkwood, ed., *Manufactured Sites: Rethinking the Post-Industrial Landscape* (London: Spon Press, 2001), 150–65. In an earlier work from 1985, Latz adopted a similar approach when he transformed Hafeninsel, a former coal shipping port in Saarbrücken, into a park. See Udo Weilacher, *Between Landscape Architecture and Land Art* (Basel: Birkhäuser, 1996).

36 For more about the relationship with Bomarzo, see the interview with Latz in Udo Weilacher, *Between Landscape Architecture and Land Art* (Basel: Birkhäuser, 1996), 128.

37 I am grateful to Bryan Fuermann for suggesting the comparison with Fountains Abbey.

38 Thomas Sieverts, "Urban Network and Townscape" in *Change without Growth: Sustainable Urban Development for the Twenty-first Century* (Braunschweig: Vieweg, 1996), 46.

39 Elizabeth K. Meyer, "The Public Park as Avant-Garde (Landscape) Architecture: A Comparative Interpretation of Two Parisian Parks, Parc de la Villette (1893–1990) and Parc des Buttes-Chaumont (1864–1867)," *Landscape Journal* 10, no. 1 (spring 1991): 16–26.

40 See Linda Pollack, "Sublime Matters: Fresh Kills," *Praxis* 4 (2002): 60.

41 For more about Crissy Field's site history and process of restoration see Kirt Rieder, "Crissy Field: Tidal Marsh Restoration and Form," in Niall Kirkwood, ed., *Manufactured Sites*, 193–207. Marc Treib discusses the transformation of Crissy Field as an excellent example of reform in accord with ecological, social, and aesthetic parameters in Treib, "Must Landscapes Mean?: Approaches to Significance in Recent Landscape Architecture," *Landscape Journal* 14, no. 1 (spring 1995): 47–62.

42 In John Beardsley, *Earthworks and Beyond: Contemporary Art in the Landscape*, 3rd ed. (New York: Abbeville Press, 1998), 193.

43 For more about Hargreaves's work at Sydney, see Ian Perlman, "Look of the Games," *Landscape Architecture* 91 (February 2001): 76–83, 97.

44 Abalos & Herreros, "Coast Park North (Park of Peace) and Installation for the Eco-Park of the Mediterranean, Barcelona, Spain, 2004," in *Metamorph Trajectories 9. International Architecture Exhibition* (New York: Rizzoli International Publications, 2004), 347. See also Abalos & Herreros, "Parc Litoral, Forum 2004, Barcelona," *2G*, no. 22 (2002): 62–69.

45 For more about this subject, see, for example, Mira Engler, "Waste Landscapes: Permissible Metaphors in Landscape Architecture," *Landscape Journal* 14, no. 1 (spring 1995): 11–25. Examples are also discussed in John Beardsley, *Earthworks and Beyond*, 166–68. A more recent example is the Hiroshima Incineration Plant, designed by Yoshio Taniguchi, which opened in 2004 and also functions as a science museum, park, and tourist destination.

46 The six finalists in the Fresh Kills competition held in 2001 were featured in *Praxis* 4 (2002): 18–63. Linda Pollack also provides an insightful and critical analysis of Field Operations' *lifescape* in Pollack, "Sublime Matters."

47 For more on this project, see Tim Richardson, ed., *The Vanguard Landscapes and Gardens of Martha Schwartz* (London: Thames & Hudson, 2004), 108–13.

48 Shlomo Aronson, *Making Peace with the Land: Designing Israel's Landscape* (Washington, D.C., and Cambridge, Mass.: Spacemaker Press, 1998), 138–39.

49 James Corner, "Not Unlike Life Itself," *Harvard Design Magazine*, no. 21 (fall 2004/winter 2005): 32.

50 Sébastien Marot, "The Return of the Landscape," in *Desvigne and Dalnoky: The Return of the Landscape* (New York: Whitney Library of Design, 1997), 9.

51 For more about Desvigne and Dalnoky's early work including the rue de Meaux courtyard see *Desvigne and Dalnoky: The Return of the Landscape* (New York: Whitney Library of Design, 1997).

52 Witold Rybczynski, *A Clearing in the Distance: Frederick Law Olmsted and America in the Nineteenth Century* (New York: Simon & Schuster, 1999), 385–86; he cites: Frederick Law Olmsted to Frederick Law Olmsted, Jr. September 5, 1890, Frederick Law Olmsted Papers, Manuscript Division, Library of Congress, Washington, D.C.

53 For a summary of this discussion see Charles Waldheim, "Landscape Urbanism: A Genealogy," *Praxis* 4 (2002): 10–17.

54 Geuze, as quoted in Bart Lootsma, "The Tradition of the New: West 8 and the Dutch Landscape," in *Het Landschap*, 88. Lootsma gives the original source for Geuze's quote as Olof Koekebakker, *Verzoening met het eigentijdse landschap, Items* 7, 1994. Lootsma has also explored the topic of landscape urbanism in "Biomorphic Intelligence and Landscape Urbanism," *Topos: European Landscape Magazine* 40 (September 2002): 10–25.

55 Waldheim, "Landscape Urbanism: A Genealogy," 13.

56 Corner, "Not Unlike Life Itself," 34.

57 On the Downsview competition, see the collection of essays assembled in Julia Czerniak, ed., *CASE: Downsview Park Toronto* (Munich: Prestel Verlag, 2001).

58 Iñaki Abalos, "Picturesque Metamorphosis," in *Metamorph Focus 9: International Architecture Exhibition*, trans. Paul Hammond (New York: Rizzoli International Publications, 2004), 149.

PROJECTS

Adriaan Geuze
**WEST 8 URBAN DESIGN &
LANDSCAPE ARCHITECTURE BV**
Rotterdam, the Netherlands

SCHOUWBURGPLEIN (Theater Square)

Rotterdam, the Netherlands 1991–96

Schouwburgplein (Theater Square), in central Rotterdam, was designed as an active public stage for temporary events and changing uses. As such, Adriaan Geuze of West 8 has reinterpreted the traditional town square as a place for public participation in unprogrammed activities rather than passive spectating. Constructed atop an underground parking garage, circumstances dictated that the surface be lightweight. For the choice of materials and overall imagery, Geuze took cues from the port city's dominant shipping industry. The plaza, slightly elevated above the surrounding area in order to create a distinct boundary, engages a nearby municipal theater, multiplex cinema, and concert hall, bringing new life to the city center.

A row of monumental, coin-operated hydraulic light masts—a kind of interactive kinetic sculpture recalling the steel cranes that unload shipping containers—is the square's signature element. By day these fantastic toylike objects perform a mechanical ballet; at night they cast pools of light on the square. The space is divided into several zones, differentiated by furniture and by economical and relatively lightweight surface materials: wood decking laid in a herringbone pattern and heavy-duty rubber (chosen because they retain heat from the sun); an epoxy floor embedded with silver maple leaves in a random pattern—a beautiful, smooth surface that has also proved popular with in-line skaters; and perforated metal floor panels that allow light from the garage below to filter through, thereby animating the ground plane at night. Jets of water located just below the metal floor panels further activate the plaza.

Pairs of ventilation stacks are lined along the northern edge of the plaza, lending definition to the open area. These towerlike structures were also designed to serve as kiosks and provide additional lighting. Directly in front of these, a single row of south-facing benches helps delineate the site. Their high, broad backrests provide a sense of protection from the surrounding streets. Due to the square's thin surface and the impossibility of planting in the ground, West 8 specified planters with flowers and a grid of large palm trees to enliven the setting in the summer.

—Peter Reed

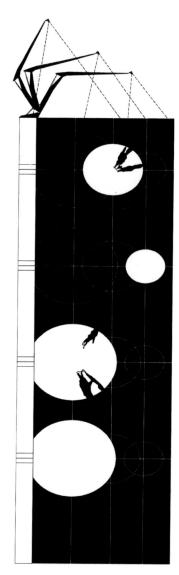

TOP: AERIAL VIEW SHOWING CONDITIONS BEFORE CONSTRUCTION

LEFT: DIAGRAMMATIC LIGHTING PLAN

AERIAL VIEW AT NIGHT

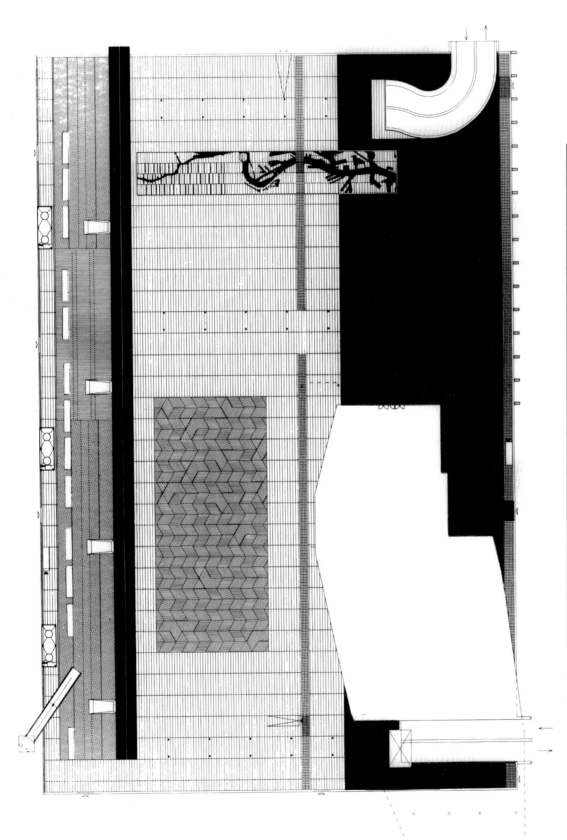

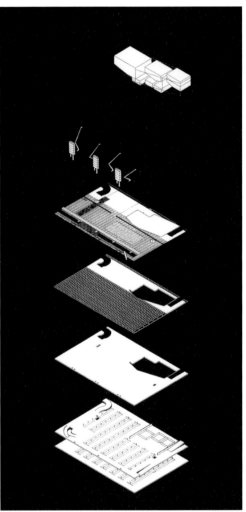

ABOVE: AXONOMETRIC DRAWING SHOWING CINEMA, LIGHT MASTS AND VENTILATION TOWERS, SQUARE SURFACE, STRUCTURE, GARAGE ROOF, AND PARKING

LEFT: PLAN

TOP: PERFORATED METAL DECK AND
HERRINGBONE-PATTERN WOOD DECK

MIDDLE: EPOXY RESIN WITH
INLAID MAPLE LEAF PATTERN

ABOVE: VIEW FROM BENCHES

TOP: EPOXY RESIN WITH INLAID MAPLE LEAF PATTERN
AND PERFORATED METAL DECK

ABOVE: FOUNTAINS IN STEEL GRATING

NIGHT VIEW

TOP: NIGHT VIEW IN THE RAIN

ABOVE: NIGHT VIEW OF ENTRANCE TO UNDERGROUND GARAGE AND
STEEL GRATING ILLUMINATED FROM BELOW

EDAW
London, England

MANCHESTER CITY CENTRE MASTER PLAN
Manchester, England 1996–present

A massive IRA terrorist bombing in 1996 destroyed over one million square feet of commercial and retail space in the heart of Manchester. The immense physical, social, and economic damage became the catalyst for revitalizing the industrial city's historic center. The city held an international competition for a bold plan that would attract people and businesses to a lively central district.

EDAW's winning master plan established a vision that not only served as a guide for rebuilding damaged structures but focused on the creation of new public spaces and significant changes to the existing street pattern and transportation network. The plan as implemented thus far has resulted in greater permeability, ease of movement, and a much-needed pedestrian network, all of which has enhanced the city center's public image while improving the physical quality of its environment and reinforcing its role as the retail heart of the region.

The plan identified locations for two new public spaces, something Manchester lacked and the community particularly wanted. One of these spaces, Exchange Square, designed by Martha Schwartz (pp. 42–47), transformed a former busy traffic intersection into a contemporary urban plaza fronted by the historic Corn Exchange, a new Marks & Spencer department store, and a remodeled shopping center. Nearby and adjacent to Manchester Cathedral, Chetham's School of Music, and the new Urbis Centre, a second new public space, City Park, replaced a parking lot with a tranquil green lawn, trees, and benches. Pedestrian paths connect these spaces to surrounding streets and Exchange Square.

The success of EDAW's far-reaching plan has led to additional improvements and developments as Manchester continues to remake its city center. Chief among these is ARUP and EDAW's complete redesign of Piccadilly Gardens (pp. 48–51), which provided Manchester with a new kind of public gathering space and principal focal point for the city.

—PR

TERRORIST BOMBING, 1996

BOMB DAMAGE, CORPORATION STREET

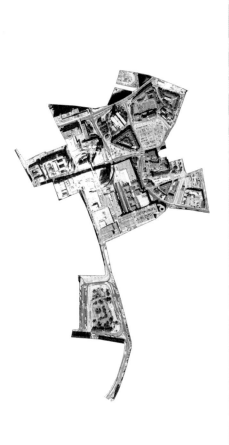

ABOVE: CITY CENTER BEFORE MASTER PLAN, WITH 1996 BOMB LOCATION HIGHLIGHTED

RIGHT: CITY CENTER AFTER MASTER PLAN

KEY
1. CHETHAM'S SCHOOL
2. CATHEDRAL
3. NEW CATHEDRAL STREET
4. MARKS & SPENCER
5. EXCHANGE SQUARE
6. CORN EXCHANGE
7. CATHEDRAL GARDEN
8. URBIS CENTRE
9. MARKET STREET
10. PICCADILLY GARDENS

Martha Schwartz
MARTHA SCHWARTZ, INC.
Cambridge, Massachusetts

EXCHANGE SQUARE

Manchester, England 1998–2000

Exchange Square, a new two-and-a-half acre pedestrian plaza, replaced a tangled traffic intersection in the heart of Manchester's central retail district. The site for such a space was identified in EDAW's master plan for Manchester (pp. 40–41), and in 1998 Martha Schwartz won an international competition with her bold, imaginative design that also reflects the city's industrial past. The irregular, triangle-shaped site, coupled with an existing topography that required level changes and a sculpting of the ground plane, posed particular design challenges, aesthetically and functionally, to accommodate the area's bustling, high-trafficked energy day and night.

Exchange Square is a hardscape with few plantings. A one-story grade change between the upper level (abutting the new Marks & Spencer department store) and the lower areas of the plaza (across from the sweeping curved facade of the historic Corn Exchange) inspired the abstract, minimalist composition of contrasting curved and straight lines that forms the plaza, which marks the juncture of the city's commercial grid with the medieval Cathedral area. Several paving materials—granite, glass, and steel in the upper area and traditional yellow pudding stone in the lower area—define these zones and enliven the overall design with chromatic and textural contrasts. A series of arced ramps framed by benches of varying length made of yellow stone seamlessly bridges the level changes of the sloping site while creating an amphitheater-like seating area. A fountain and water channel paved with irregular slate blocks cut an arc across the lower edge of the square. The fountain, with its stepping stones, traces the historic Hanging Ditch watercourse that once flowed through the old city. In the upper plaza flush-mounted railroad tracks with bright blue flatbed benches lyrically refer to the historical importance of railroads in Manchester. Punctuated with in-ground lighting, the stylized track beds glow at night.

Not all of Schwartz's plan was realized. Originally, she envisioned a group of historic artifacts displayed like archaeological objets trouvés in shadow boxes embedded in the walls. A more whimsical gesture on a grander scale was her proposal for rows of artificial metallic palm trees "planted" on the upper level. Functionally, they would have formed a gate for pedestrians and cars; sculpturally, they would have imparted a festive atmosphere not unlike the famous cast-iron columns with painted copper palm leaves in the Great Kitchen of Brighton's Royal Pavilion, designed by John Nash in the early nineteenth century.

—PR

COMPETITION DRAWING WITH ARTIFICIAL PALM TREES

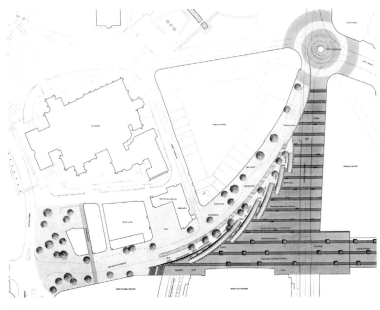

PLAN

FLATBED RAILWAY BENCHES AND STONE BENCHES

FLATBED RAILWAY BENCHES ON STYLIZED TRACK BEDS

AERIAL VIEW AFTER REDEVELOPMENT

AERIAL VIEW

TOP: HANGING DITCH FOUNTAIN

ABOVE: GENERAL VIEW WITH HANGING DITCH FOUNTAIN IN FOREGROUND

VIEW OF RAMPS AND STONE BENCHES

ARUP
Manchester, England

EDAW
London, England

PICCADILLY GARDENS
Manchester, England 1998–2002

Traditionally the heart of Manchester and one of the city center's few green spaces, Piccadilly Gardens was formerly a sunken garden of ornamental plantings and cherry trees that had become a characterless no-man's-land. Choked off from the city by the overwhelming pressure of the surrounding transportation infrastructure, the decline of the gardens was further exacerbated by vacancies in nearby buildings. Based on the success of EDAW's master plan for Manchester (pp. 40–41), the city commissioned ARUP and EDAW to completely redesign Piccadilly as a modern urban park measuring thirteen-and-a-half acres that would serve as the city's principal public space. Piccadilly Gardens provides a new focal point in the city center: a place to meet, relax, and congregate in an attractive, accessible setting close to transportation networks.

The main elements of ARUP and EDAW's design create a space that is open, light, and flexible: a broad central lawn, a monumental fountain, a pavilion, and changes to the adjacent tramline and roadways. The possibilities for vegetation are limited due to the

extensive underground infrastructure (including an electrical substation and pump house), but the park is enlivened with seasonal change by means of relatively modest plantings, such as spring crocuses that transform an entire area into a swath of purple.

Fountain Plaza, a central feature placed at an angle to the street grid, takes the form of a tilted oval disk of black granite surrounded by a ring of mist and 180 computer-controlled aerated jets that rise and fall in a lively display of water and light. The fountain is fully accessible and, unsurprisingly, has become a popular place to play. A principal pedestrian thoroughfare bridges the fountain and forms a straight line across the width of the park. This so-called catwalk provides a place for promenading and people-watching and creates a sense of public theater new to Manchester.

Another major pedestrian path, paved in high-quality sandstone, cuts an arc across the lawn, connecting opposite corners of the park. The path's curved axis is echoed in the minimalist geometry of the one-story concrete pavilion designed by Tadao Ando. Ando's pavilion, which houses a café and an information center, and a new commercial building by Allies & Morrison are sited along two edges of the park to help reduce the impact of the heavily trafficked surrounding streets and adjacent bus station. At one end of the park, sections of redundant tramline and roadway were replaced by new paving, seating, and a grove of fastigiate oak trees, effectively extending the park to the edge of the surrounding buildings.

—PR

AERIAL VIEW BEFORE CONSTRUCTION

NIGHT VIEW OF NEW GROVE OF TREES AND SEATING AREA

AERIAL VIEW AFTER CONSTRUCTION

LEFT: VIEW ACROSS PARK TOWARD
MARKET STREET

ABOVE LEFT AND RIGHT: VIEW OF FOUNTAIN AND ONE-STORY PAVILION DESIGNED
BY TADAO ANDO

AERIAL VIEW OF CATWALK AND FOUNTAIN

VIEW OF TRAMLINE AND ROADWAY BEFORE
CONSTRUCTION

VIEW OF REDESIGNED TRAMLINE AND ROADWAY WITH
NEW GROVE OF TREES AND SEATING AREA

ALSOP LTD
London, England

BRADFORD CITY CENTRE MASTER PLAN
Bradford, England 2003; projected completion, 2020

The city of Bradford, in northern England, is rethinking itself: the changing economic base from manufacturing to services and deeply rooted social issues that culminated in race riots during the mid-1990s have led civic-minded individuals from both the public and private sectors to find ways to revitalize the city and improve quality of life. Alsop Ltd has set forth a twenty-year vision to promote new development by improving the public realm. Unlike many urban-planning initiatives, which add buildings to the city fabric, Bradford's plan calls for the demolition of buildings to create a large park connecting several neighborhoods to the city center, where no significant public space had previously existed.

Bradford experienced dispersed development until 1955, when the construction of a ring road confined development to its center. These postwar buildings now stand largely vacant. By removing such undesirable structures and phasing out the unsuccessful and only partially completed ring road, the new master plan reveals the area's topography and waterways that brought the city to prominence as a textile center during the Industrial Revolution. The centerpiece of the design is the new Bradford Bowl, a large artificial lake that partially surrounds City Hall. Situated where two valleys converge, the city center is the natural drainage point of North Brook and Bradford Beck. The designers call for releasing these two watercourses from underground culverts to flow through the new park, highlighting the natural resources from which the city draws its name (Broad Ford).

The designers analyzed and responded to the areas immediately adjacent to the park, reshaping the existing neighborhoods into three new areas: the Market, the Valley, and the Channel. Even within these areas, the designers systematically examined local conditions to help them shape the park's various elements. Gardens provide gathering space around the mosque in the Market. Wetlands, orchards, and playgrounds in the Valley supplement educational programs at nearby Bradford College and the University of Bradford. Recreational fields running along the rebuilt Leeds-Liverpool Canal allow programmed activities in the new residential and retail Channel neighborhood.

The master plan is a social response as much as it is a design solution. Site analysis revealed that none of Bradford's communities occupied the center and inhabitants tended to identify themselves with their neighborhood districts rather than the city as a whole. The park connects formerly separated quarters in an effort to integrate the communities. By providing open space and allowing people to gather, the city hopes that the increased pedestrian traffic will encourage new retail and entertainment activities to develop around this area over time.

The Bradford City Council adopted the plan in March 2004 and demolition of buildings in the existing Broadway retail area in the Channel commenced in April 2004. The new retail area is scheduled for completion by April 2005. Bradford Centre Regeneration is actively acquiring new properties that have been earmarked for demolition. Though Alsop's renderings here include iconoclastic and Pop-infused buildings, the actual development will take shape as sites become available to developers and architects over time.

—Irene Shum

VIEW OF BROADWAY BEFORE DEMOLITION

RENDERING OF PROPOSED NEW PARK AND REDEVELOPMENT OF
BROADWAY IN CHANNEL AREA

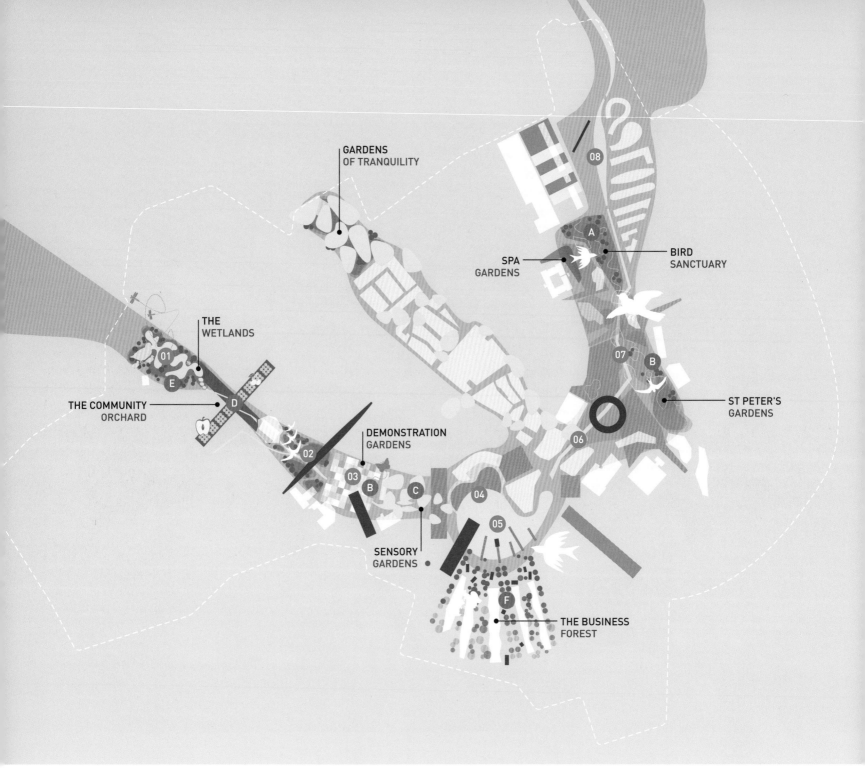

GARDENS
OF TRANQUILITY

SPA
GARDENS

BIRD
SANCTUARY

THE
WETLANDS

01

E

ST PETER'S
GARDENS

THE COMMUNITY
ORCHARD

D

07

B

06

02

DEMONSTRATION
GARDENS

03

B

C

04

05

SENSORY
GARDENS

F

THE BUSINESS
FOREST

08

A

DIAGRAMMATIC PLAN OF NEW PUBLIC OPEN SPACES
AND GARDENS IN CITY CENTER

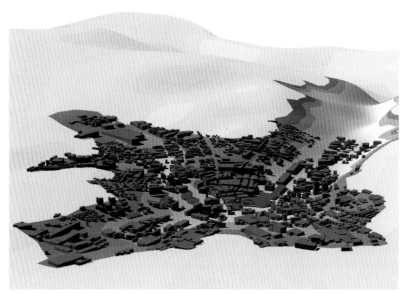

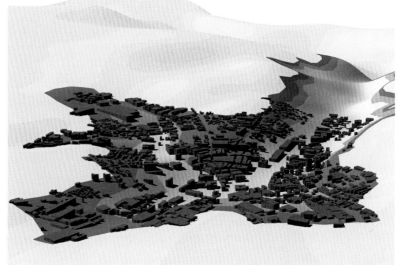

RENDERING OF EXISTING URBAN FABRIC, SHOWING BUILDINGS TO BE DEMOLISHED

RENDERING OF NEW CITY CENTER

ABOVE: VIEW OF BROADWAY BEFORE DEMOLITION

RIGHT: RENDERING OF FIRST PHASE OF PROPOSED
BROADWAY REDEVELOPMENT

ABOVE: EXISTING VIEW OF CHANNEL AREA

RIGHT: RENDERING OF PROPOSED CHANNEL AREA, LOCATED ALONG
REINSTATED LEEDS-LIVERPOOL CANAL

ABOVE: AERIAL VIEW OF CITY HALL AND EXISTING CITY FABRIC

RIGHT: RENDERING OF PROPOSED BRADFORD BOWL AND CITY HALL

ABOVE: EXISTING VIEW OF VALLEY AREA

RIGHT: RENDERING OF PROPOSED VALLEY AREA

Peter Walker
**PETER WALKER WILLIAM JOHNSON
AND PARTNERS**
Berkeley, California

Masayuki Kusumoto
NTT URBAN DEVELOPMENT CO.
Tokyo, Japan

Yoji Sasaki
**OHTORI CONSULTANTS
ENVIRONMENTAL DESIGN INSTITUTE**
Osaka, Japan

KEYAKI PLAZA   Saitama New Urban Center
Saitama City, Japan 1994–2000

Keyaki Plaza, a contemporary version of the traditional town square, is situated on the roof of a commercial building at the heart of Saitama Prefecture's new urban center. Encompassing more than one hundred acres and built on a former rail yard, the center includes a new sports arena, government office buildings, and commuter train station. The plaza, elevated twenty-seven feet above ground-level shops and cafés and accessed by ramps, stairs, and elevators, is a remarkable achievement technically, aesthetically, and symbolically. The landscape architects worked closely with the building's architect, NTT Urban Development, to realize their goals.

The plaza is based on the symbolic idea of transplanting a grove of trees from a nearby temple complex into the new urban infrastructure. More than two hundred zelkova trees (*keyaki* in Japanese), arranged in a grid, are planted in a section of earth, which is visible on the facades of the building's glass curtain wall. The concept evokes Walter de Maria's famous *Earth Room* but here the design is given significant hydroponic properties. Unlike most plazas, which are graded for drainage, the surface at Keyaki is truly flat so that rainwater irrigates the earth below the perforated metal paving.

The choice of zelkova trees in large measure gives the plaza its identity. They are an evident symbol of the nearby Hikawa Shrine, where they line the ceremonial way to the site. At Keyaki Plaza the trees are planted in a modular grid consonant with the architecture, but the unmistakable reference to Hikawa is appropriate for a site that is intended to be a quiet refuge from the city. The dimensions of the paving and the placement of trees and furniture are rigorously controlled so that the reductive space reads as flat and calm as this Minimalist composition. The floor of cast aluminum and granite pavers can be seen as the building's fifth elevation in that the roof responds to the all-over rhythm of the curtain wall grid. The square wood-and-glass benches, illuminated at night like lanterns, are carefully integrated into the module without destroying the experience of the flat plane. Within this controlled composition, the trees are allowed to retain their natural individuality—a welcome contrast to the building's orthogonal geometry.

Restraint is applied to other sections of the plaza as well. A sunken area occasionally serves as a performance space and is distinguished by a surface of round glass blocks that, by day, serve as skylights for the space below. When lit at night, the blocks transform the space into a glowing horizontal screen. The lawn, which provides a chromatic and textural counterpoint to the paving, was the designers' response to the program for a children's play area. It extends the flat ground plane and is consonant with the desire for a visually quiet environment.

—PR

ABOVE: HIKAWA SHRINE, SAITAMA CITY

RIGHT: CEREMONIAL ROUTE TO HIKAWA SHRINE
LINED WITH ZELKOVA TREES

VIEW OF PLAZA WITH LAWN FOR CHILDREN'S PLAYGROUND

AERIAL VIEW OF KEYAKI PLAZA

FAR LEFT: SUNKEN PLAZA AT NIGHT

LEFT: AERIAL VIEW OF SUNKEN PLAZA
SHOWING CONCRETE AND
GLASS SURFACE

STAIRCASE WITH RAMPED FOUNTAIN LEADING TO PLAZA; "EARTH ROOM"
HIGHLIGHTED BY TRANSLUCENT GLASS CURTAIN WALL

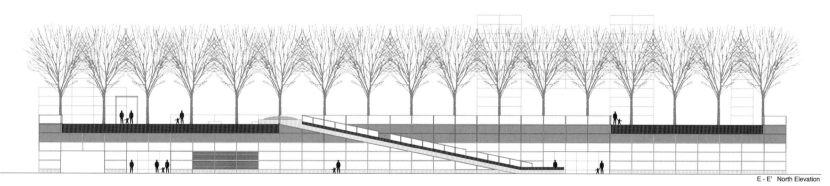

E - E' North Elevation

NORTH ELEVATION

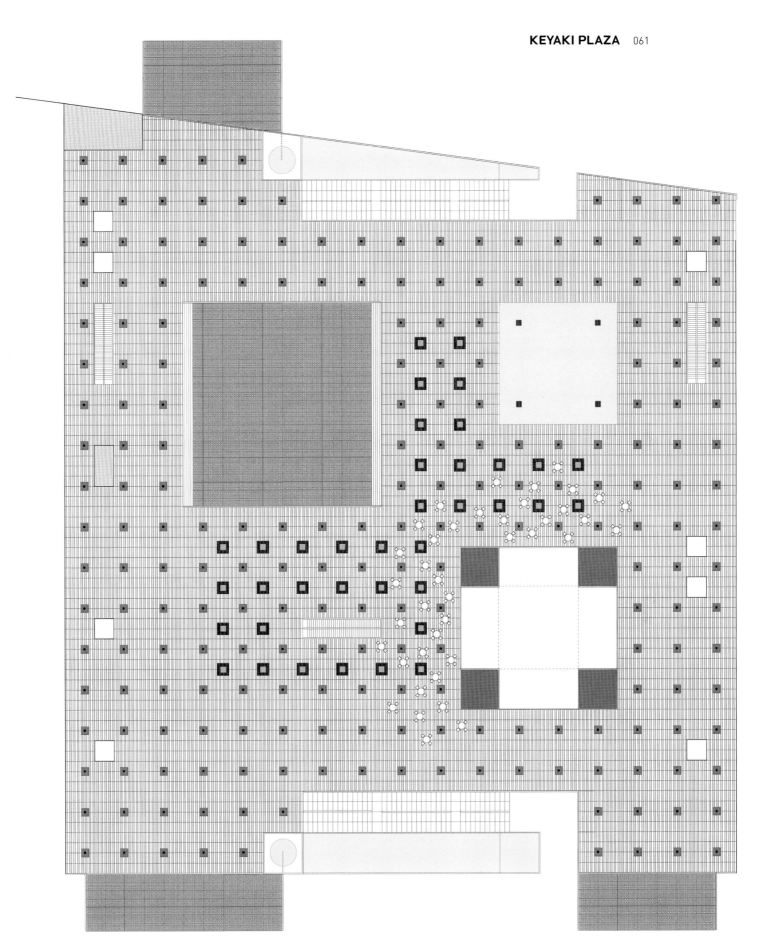

PLAN

VIEW IN SUMMER

VIEW IN WINTER

AERIAL VIEW IN SUMMER

AERIAL VIEW IN AUTUMN

Tom Leader
TOM LEADER STUDIO
Berkeley, California

Michael Duncan
SKIDMORE, OWINGS & MERRILL LLP
San Francisco, California

SHANGHAI CARPET Shanghai Yang Pu University City Hub

Shanghai, China 2003; projected completion, 2006

Like an intricately cut gem set to its best advantage, Tom Leader's Shanghai Carpet—a richly textured plaza—forms the central outdoor spine of Shanghai Yang Pu University City Hub, a new state-of-the-art development with high-tech steel and glass buildings designed by Skidmore, Owings & Merrill. The Hub is the focal point of Shanghai's rapidly developing Yang Pu district, where it will serve as the area's center for commerce, innovation, and technological research. The Hub is an important link between major public transportation systems, University City, with its numerous campuses, and the historic Jiang Wan Stadium nearby.

The principal outdoor space, designed by Tom Leader, is a T-shaped sunken pedestrian plaza. A network of stairs, landscaped ramps, and escalators links the street level to the shops and plaza that cover a large underground parking garage below. In contrast to the surrounding modern architecture, the plaza is designed with relatively humble materials associated with daily life in Shanghai as it existed for centuries, including stone, brick, and timber recycled from China's Yellow River Gorge project. As such, the plaza suggests an excavation or digging back into time.

Running the length of the plaza is the 650-foot-long Shanghai Carpet. The composition is treated like a collage, so that walking the length of the "carpet" gives a changing sequence of experiences, which the designer describes as a "jump-cutting series of textures ranging from the richness of a traditional Chinese garden to the urban street quality of Shanghai." The assemblage of materials, minimal plantings, and fountains breaks up the linear expanse. Juxtaposed with the rustic materials, a long, narrow LED screen displaying data cuts through the entire length of the carpet flush with the ground, like a runnel in a traditional garden. This modern stream is intended as a venue for Chinese digital and electronic artists and poets who will be asked to create an inventory of programs based on themes tied to specific times of the day and year.

Because the plaza is built on slab, there are limited opportunities for planting. Timber bamboo, which requires little soil, lines one edge of the plaza, its slender stems and delicate leaves providing dappled shade without blocking views of the adjacent storefronts. Ferns and mosses will be planted among the stones and other paving materials, and small trees and vines such as wisteria have also been selected to soften the hardscape of the sunken area.

—PR

URBAN PLAN

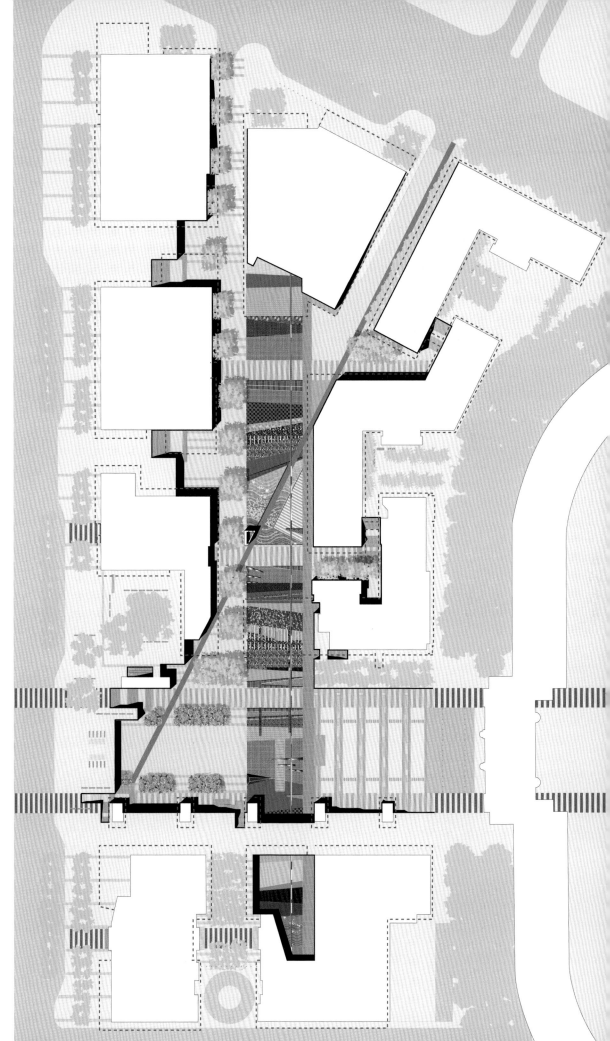

SITE PLAN

COLLAGE OF TRADITIONAL TEXTURES
AND MATERIALS

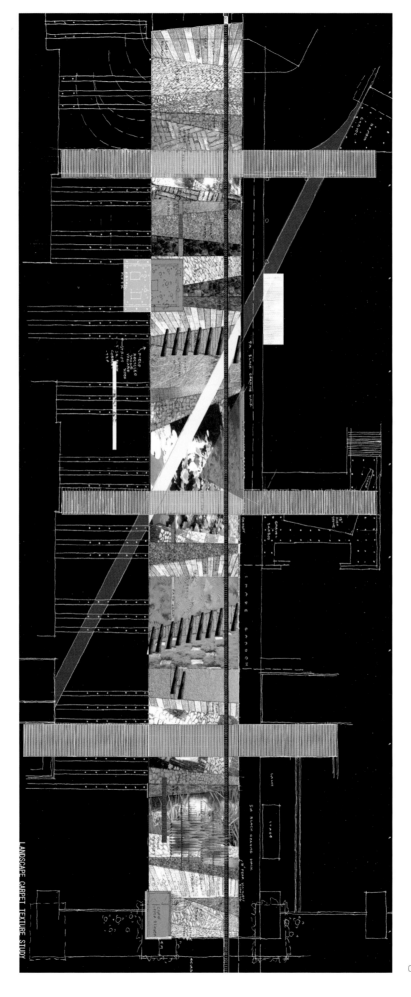

LANDSCAPE CARPET TEXTURE STUDY

CONCEPT PLAN OF SHANGHAI CARPET

LEFT: RENDERINGS OF PLAZA

OPPOSITE: EXPLODED AXONOMETRIC VIEW OF UNIVERSITY
HUB WITH PRINCIPAL CIRCULATION DIAGRAM

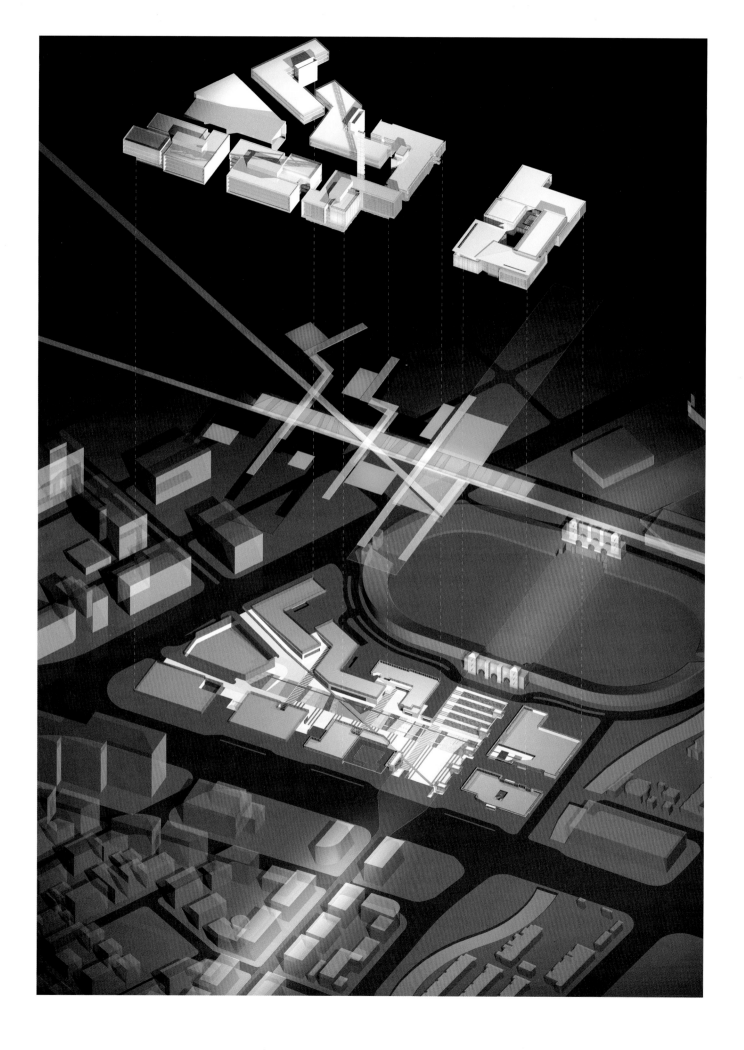

Christophe Girot
ATELIER PHUSIS
Paris, France

INVALIDENPARK

Berlin, Germany 1992–97

In redesigning Invalidenpark, in central Berlin, Christophe Girot was faced with creating meaningful yet appropriate public space on a site with a complex history and military associations dating back to Prussia. Like other projects undertaken as part of the reconstruction of Berlin following German reunification, the emotionally charged issue of how to acknowledge the past yet build for the future in the newly reinstituted capital came to the fore.

Prior to Girot's design, the park had undergone several transformations since the eighteenth century. It began as a formal, symmetrically planned military parade ground, then in 1843 was made over into a romanticized wooded memorial park designed by Peter Joseph Lenné. A neo–Gothic Revival memorial chapel was added in 1891 to commemorate the Franco-Prussian War. Destroyed during World War II, the chapel's foundations lay beneath the surface when the ruined park served the East German secret police as a makeshift staging area for border control, one block from the Berlin Wall and the Invalidenstrasse checkpoint. Rather than dwelling on these historical associations, however, Girot emphasizes the site's value as an open space for public use and enjoyment.

The park's most striking feature is *Sinking Wall*, a dramatic sculpture at its center. Visible from the streets surrounding the park, the wall is a large triangular form that appears to be dissolving into the shallow basin surrounding it. Both the basin and sculpture are offset from the park's original north-south axis and are placed on an angle, facing the neighboring square. Traces of the old chapel's foundations can be found at the base of the wall, where a ramp climbs up the spine of the sculpture to an unobstructed view of the sky. Although the obvious reference is the Berlin Wall, the sculpture does not share the same shape or material as the original wall. Without knowing its name or the history of the site, the sculpture would read simply as a modern, minimal fountain. For Girot, "The narrative is hidden in the abstraction of the wedge."

The site is divided into north and south sections. The north side is wooded and contains several oak trees from the original park. The south side, off Invalidenstrasse, is a small sunken plaza. The transition from north to south is a series of gradually broadening alternating bands of lawn and paving. The entire ground plane is tilted by one degree; the slope is almost imperceptible except at the park's edges, where it creates a distinct border requiring the visitor to either step down or step up when entering or exiting, making manifest the delicate balance between past and present. The large shallow basin surrounding *Sinking Wall* is the park's only level surface, creating a distinct frame around the sculpture. In front of the basin to the south are gingko trees, ancient symbols of hope and perseverance.

—IS

INVALIDENPARK AND GNADENKIRCHE, 1930

INVALIDENPARK DURING COLD WAR, UNDATED
PHOTOGRAPH, POST-1967

VIEW FROM NORTHEAST TOWARD INVALIDENSTRASSE

VIEW FROM NORTHWEST TOWARD INVALIDENSTRASSE

ABOVE LEFT: ENTRANCE FROM INVALIDENSTRASSE
TO SUNKEN PLAZA

ABOVE: VIEW FROM *SINKING WALL*

COMPETITION PLAN

TOP: VIEW FROM EAST

ABOVE: VIEW OF *SINKING WALL* AT NIGHT

TOP: VIEW OF *SINKING WALL* TOWARD INVALIDENSTRASSE

ABOVE: AERIAL VIEW FROM INVALIDENSTRASSE

Kathryn Gustafson and
Neil Porter
GUSTAFSON PORTER LTD
London, England

HADIQAT AS-SAMAH (Garden of Forgiveness)
Beirut Central District, Beirut, Lebanon 2000; projected completion, 2006

In 2000, Gustafson Porter Ltd was selected from an invited competition to design Hadiqat As-Samah, the Garden of Forgiveness, in Beirut. Located within the historic core of the city, the 5.7-acre site is an agglomeration of several city blocks destroyed during the country's sixteen-year civil war that ended in 1991. Due to the ensuing damage, archaeologists were able to excavate the site, discovering building and street foundations from several periods of history dating from antiquity to the Middle Ages. Surrounded by seven different houses of worship, the site and its ruins suggest a shared heritage of cultural diversity, long predating the differences that caused recent conflict.

Hadiqat As-Samah follows a long tradition of allegorical gardens in the Middle East. For the designers, an old children's puzzle containing a map of Lebanon that was found while gathering research for the competition inspired their vision. In the words of Neil Porter, the "piecing together of the puzzle symbolized the journey that Lebanon had embarked upon to become unified and prosperous." Plants were selected to represent the various regions of modern Lebanon, from the mountains to the Mediterranean coast. This is especially evident in the upper section—the lush Paradise Garden—where the main entrance is located.

After entering, visitors cross a large rectangular pool and continue down a wide ramp flanked by terraces. The upper terrace contains plants from the mountain regions, such as Judas trees, the agricultural plains are represented in the middle level with olive groves, and citrus trees from the coastal plain are found at the bottom level.

At the end of the ramp is Visitor's Square, where one can enter either the visitor's center or the archaeological garden. The visitor's center is tucked underneath the adjacent street and does not protrude into the garden. The designer references the Roman cardo (main north-south road) and decumanus (east-west road) by creating strong linear axes in the archaeological garden, while ancient building foundations define rooms within the garden. Herbs used in Roman medicine and cooking and plants used to produce pigment for dyeing textiles are among the vegetation that fills the rooms. Their shallow root structures will not compromise the archaeological foundations underneath. A pergola extends across much of the south side of the garden to protect the bedrock on which Hellenistic ruins sit, as well as to provide shade for visitors. Medieval streets are mapped onto the pergola, allowing traces of these ancient paths to be seen in shadow form under the midday sun. Growing onto and over the pergola will be climbing roses, a flower that originated in the Middle East.

Hadiqat As-Samah is the city's first public garden. Although it is enclosed, there are no freestanding walls surrounding it. Instead, its periphery is made up of the foundations of the adjoining pedestrian streets and religious buildings. The garden represents an effort to rebuild the city, both physically and symbolically, and to create a site that reflects the country's sense of postwar reconciliation and healing. Accessible to all, one needs not an invitation or a particular religious or political affiliation to enjoy this verdant space in the heart of the capital.

—IS

AERIAL VIEW OF SITE FROM SOUTHWEST

SITE PLAN

PHOTOMONTAGE OF EXISTING SITE FROM NORTHWEST

PHOTOMONTAGE OF EXISTING SITE FROM ST. GEORGE'S
MARONITE CATHEDRAL

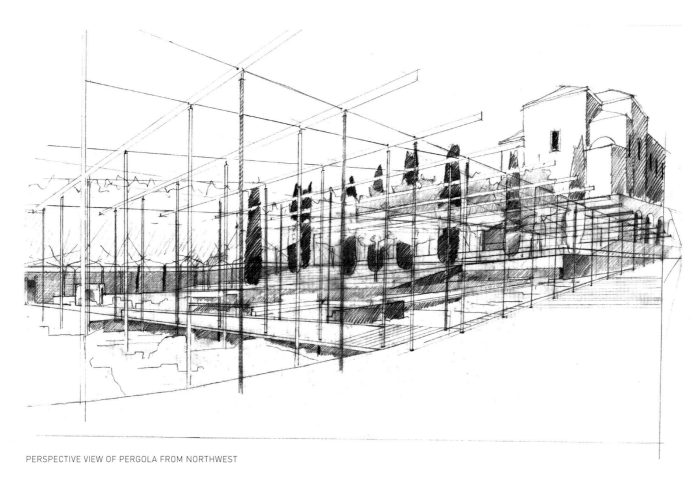

PERSPECTIVE VIEW OF PERGOLA FROM NORTHWEST

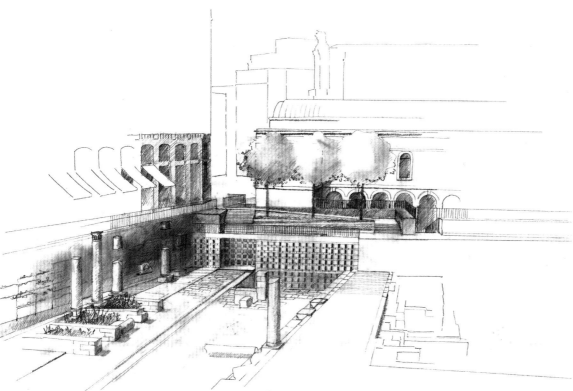

PERSPECTIVE VIEW OF ARCHAEOLOGICAL GARDEN FROM SOUTH

metaphors for unity

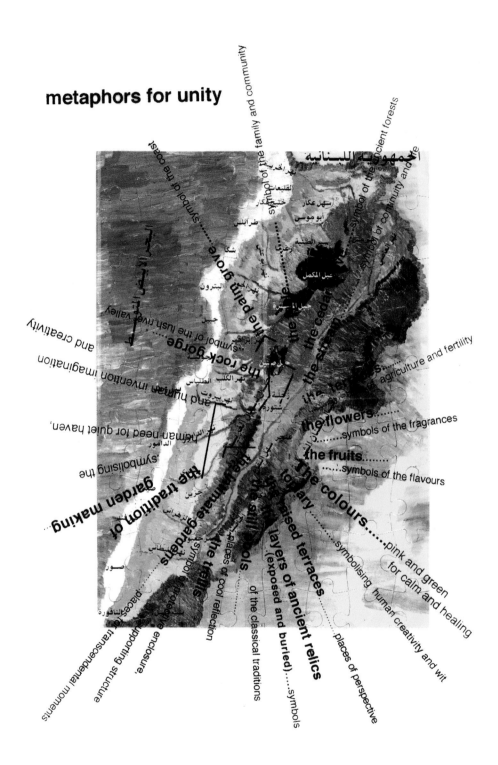

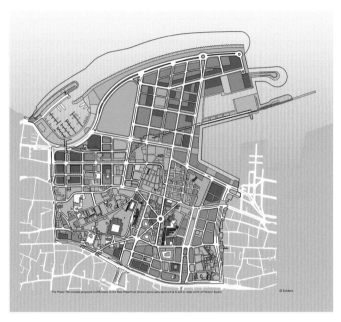

ABOVE: PLAN OF BEIRUT'S CENTRAL DISTRICT

LEFT: CONCEPTUAL STUDY, CHILDREN'S PUZZLE WITH ANNOTATIONS

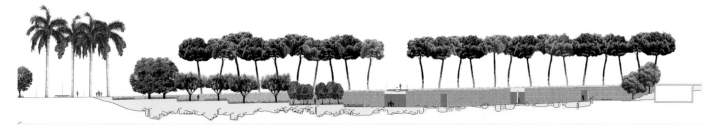

1. SECTION THROUGH TERRACES LOOKING EAST TO VISITOR'S CENTER

2. SECTION THROUGH PARADISE GARDEN LOOKING NORTH TOWARD ENTRANCE

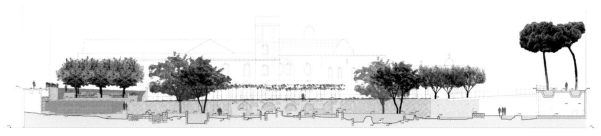

3. SECTION THROUGH ROMAN SETTLEMENT LOOKING NORTH

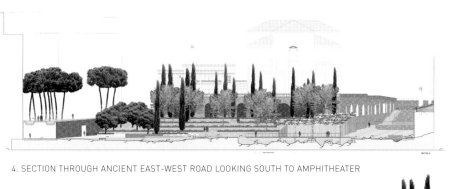

4. SECTION THROUGH ANCIENT EAST-WEST ROAD LOOKING SOUTH TO AMPHITHEATER

5. SECTION THROUGH PERGOLA LOOKING EAST

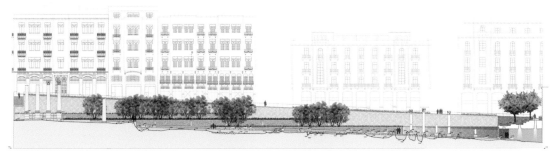

6. SECTION THROUGH ANCIENT NORTH-SOUTH ROAD LOOKING WEST

Ken Smith
KEN SMITH LANDSCAPE ARCHITECT
New York, New York

THE MUSEUM OF MODERN ART ROOF GARDEN
New York, New York 2003–05

Rather than settle for an ordinary surface of black and white stone ballast, The Museum of Modern Art recognized an opportunity for a more creative and imaginative roof garden atop its new building designed by Yoshio Taniguchi in midtown Manhattan. However, the program for the rooftop above the sixth-floor exhibition galleries on the north and south sides of the Museum came with a long list of restrictions: live plants were strongly discouraged; the need for water was to be minimized or eliminated altogether; the height of the landscape could not exceed approximately three feet; there were limitations as to the amount of load the roof could support; and white stones (roof ballast) should ideally be incorporated in the design because the client had already purchased the material prior to the garden commission. Also, there is no public access; this is a garden to be viewed from afar. In fact, visitors to the Museum would never see the roof garden. Only people in the surrounding buildings would enjoy a view from above of this unconventional setting for a contemporary art project.

Ken Smith's design plays with the pattern of camouflage, as much for its aesthetic potential as for its associations with nature, simulation, and urban culture.

Drawing on a palette of white roof ballast, artificial rocks, crushed glass, recycled black rubber, artificial boxwood, and a green plastic supporting armature, the materials are arranged in an organic pattern to imitate camouflage. Rather than providing any concealment, the seemingly free-form design is a striking contrast with the controlled, orthogonal geometry of Taniguchi's architecture and of Philip Johnson's Abby Aldrich Rockefeller Sculpture Garden visible below. The camouflage here, as in other aspects of contemporary youth culture, calls attention to itself. As Smith explains, he intends his project to take "the art of camouflage and the artifice of simulation a step further by using the simulation itself as a source for design speculation. One might think of this as the simulation of a simulation or using imitated nature to generate a new nature."

By playing with notions of the artificial and natural, Smith points to the fact that much of landscape design recalls an ideal nature but is in fact a highly artificial construct intended to conceal what lies below or beyond. Given the highly artificial environment and limitations of the setting, it seems fitting to impose the imagery of imitated nature onto a built construction.

—PR

SOUTH GARDEN LOOKING WEST ALONG 53RD STREET

ROOF GARDEN MATERIALS

BLACK RECYCLED
RUBBER

WHITE STONES

CRUSHED GLASS

FOAM HEADER

FIBERGLASS GRATING

SHRUB ASSEMBLY

BLACK ARTIFICIAL
ROCK

WHITE ARTIFICIAL
ROCK

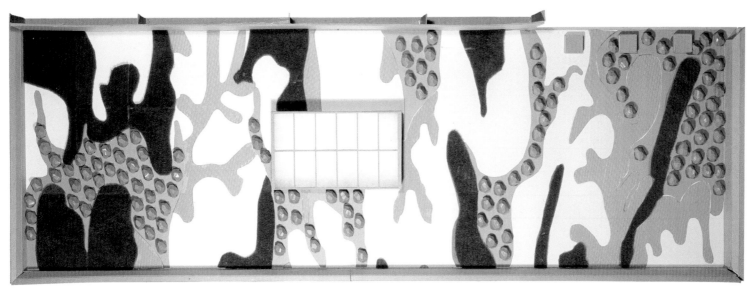

STUDY MODEL OF SOUTH GARDEN

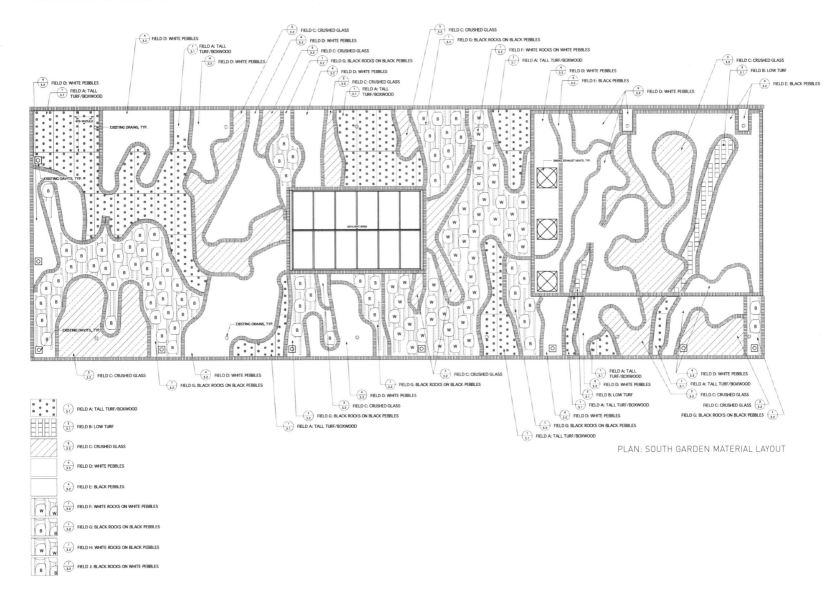

PLAN: SOUTH GARDEN MATERIAL LAYOUT

FIELD A: TALL TURF/BOXWOOD
FIELD B: LOW TURF
FIELD C: CRUSHED GLASS
FIELD D: WHITE PEBBLES
FIELD E: BLACK PEBBLES
FIELD F: WHITE ROCKS ON WHITE PEBBLES
FIELD G: BLACK ROCKS ON BLACK PEBBLES
FIELD H: WHITE ROCKS ON BLACK PEBBLES
FIELD J: BLACK ROCKS ON WHITE PEBBLES

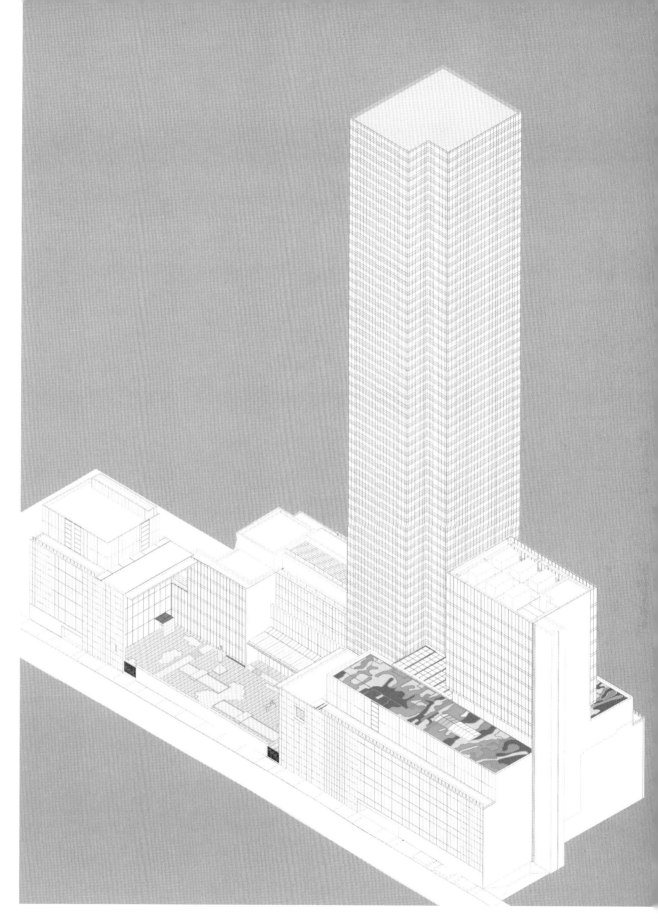

AXONOMETRIC VIEW FROM NORTHWEST

Catherine Mosbach
MOSBACH PAYSAGISTES
Paris, France

BORDEAUX BOTANICAL GARDEN

La Bastide, Bordeaux, France 2000–02

The new Bordeaux Botanical Garden, designed by Catherine Mosbach, is a research facility for the study of natural resource management and biodiversity. Located in La Bastide, the recently converted mixed-use neighborhood in Bordeaux's former industrial right bank, the garden sits prominently on axis with the city's main public square, Place des Quinconces, across the river. Potentially difficult due to its long, thin configuration (approximately 2,000 by 230 feet) and flat terrain, Mosbach masterfully organized the area into successive gardens, drawing visitors from the active Garonne Riverfront into the new residential-education area. Melding art with science, Mosbach creates moments of repose and beauty throughout the site.

The garden is arranged by growing condition rather than plant family. There are three main areas: a water garden, the Environment Gallery, and the Field of Crops. Together these areas represent the environmental characteristics of the surrounding Aquitaine Basin. The sequence progresses from plants that grow in water and do not require soil to naturally occurring soil structures and textures from the habitats in the region to highly controlled, cultivated fields. The water garden, along the western edge, separates the site from the busy quay. Over two and a half acres, the large pool reflects the sky, expanding the garden beyond its tight urban plot and creating a serene atmosphere. Irregularly shaped paths run along the perimeter into the pool, allowing visitors to walk among the water plants.

In order for scientists to study natural processes, Mosbach had to recreate nature. This is most dramatically exemplified in the Environment Gallery where eleven separate landscapes represent regional habitats, from the sand dunes of the Bay of Biscay to limestone hills. The topography for each landscape is shaped by its natural substrate and soil makeup. Unlike in nature, however, here the geologic strata sit atop the ground plane, on view for visitors to see. Walking among the landscapes, the topographic changes reveal the rock and soil components of each particular habitat. The shared palette of neutral tones and natural materials allows the eye to connect the strata of the various landscapes, creating a unified composition.

In sharp contrast to the Environment Gallery, the rational and geometric pattern of the Field of Crops reflects planned, careful cultivation. Each plot has a separate irrigation system, providing maximum control. The elongated plots of each crop exaggerate the overall site's length. By constructing and controlling the variable soil conditions, researchers can focus on how plants grow and adapt. For Mosbach, "These ungrounded gardens, set alongside each other, combine together by an optical effect to create a general landscape....This is truly dreamlike, these palpable collages that are meaningful."

—IS

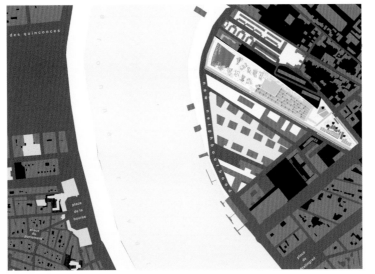

SITE PLAN

VIEW OF FIELD OF CROPS

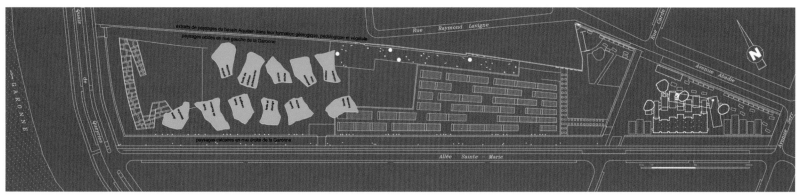

TOP: ELEVATIONS AND SECTIONS OF ENVIRONMENT GALLERY

ABOVE: PLAN OF GARDEN WITH ENVIRONMENT GALLERY IN GREEN

DETAIL OF DUNE HINTERLAND HABITAT IN
ENVIRONMENT GALLERY

BELOW: VIEW FROM ENVIRONMENT GALLERY
TOWARD WEST

VIEW OF ENVIRONMENT GALLERY

VIEW FROM WATER GARDEN TOWARD ENVIRONMENT GALLERY

AERIAL VIEW OF WATER GARDEN LOOKING TOWARD GARONNE RIVER

DETAIL OF WATER GARDEN

Kathryn Gustafson
PAYSAGE LAND
Paris, France

VALODE & PISTRE ARCHITECTES
Paris, France

SHELL PETROLEUM HEADQUARTERS
Rueil-Malmaison, France 1989–91

For the Shell Petroleum Headquarters (now Schneider Electric) in suburban Paris, Kathryn Gustafson designed an innovative landscape seamlessly integrated and coordinated with Valode & Pistre's new architecture on the six-acre site. Aesthetically and symbolically the gardens create a unique environment and formal counterpoint to the modernist, low-rise buildings of steel, stone, and glass and, where necessary, the landscape shields and even conceals the corporate offices from the surrounding residential neighborhood.

The entry presents a series of particularly striking images metaphoric of rolling countryside. To one side of the entry plaza contours of lawn unfold in waves of green. The sculpted berms, seductive in their own right and evocative of hills and other organic forms, conceal an underground parking structure and utility building. The sloping lawn is incised by limestone walls that accommodate access stairs and ventilation shafts for the underground garage. These architectural elements contrast rhythmically, formally, and chromatically with the undulating lawn in this minimalist composition.

A large, austere reflecting pool, punctuated by four stainless steel light masts that resemble giant drill bits, borders the other side of the entry plaza. Taken together, the lawn and pool loosely symbolize earth and water, reflecting Shell's ongoing exploration for natural resources. Water from the pool flows under the entry rotunda and cascades into the colorful aquatic garden full of plants and flowering shrubs. The narrow water channel, constructed on slab, divides a principal office wing from the personnel services building. The moatlike pool is viewed from overhead bridges and from the glazed corridors and cafeteria of the flanking buildings.

A series of pocket gardens occupies the spaces between office wings. Each garden, planted with trees, shrubs, and grasses, is given a unique identity based in part on color. In the white garden, beds of roses are juxtaposed with rippling planes of grass and columns of trees that echo the building's pilotis and screen office bays from each other. In the yellow garden, beds of perennial plants and trees share a similar compositional strategy but with a different effect and mood. In other gardens reds and blues dominate. The entire landscape was designed as much out of consideration for the employees' daily experience as to convey a distinctive and memorable company image and experience to their visitors.

—PR

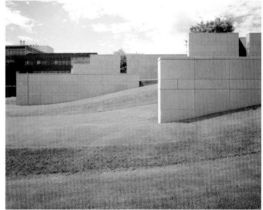

TOP AND ABOVE: LAWN OVER PARKING GARAGE WITH
LIMESTONE WALLS FOR FIRE STAIRS

VIEW OF POOL AND LAWN FROM LOBBY

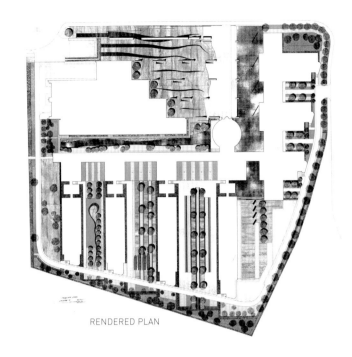

RENDERED PLAN

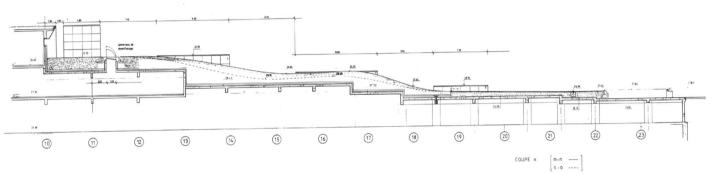

COUPE n [m-n ———]
        [n-o -----]

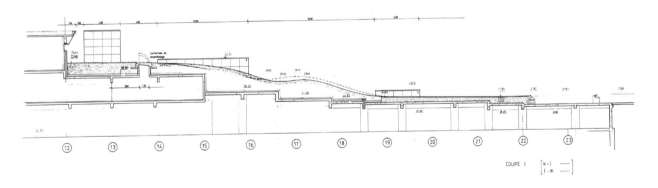

COUPE l [k-l ———]
        [l-m -----]

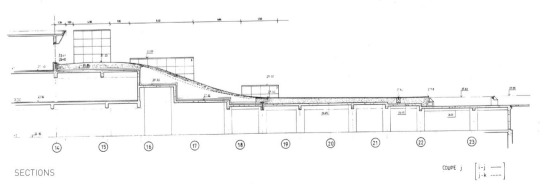

SECTIONS

COUPE j [i-j ———]
        [j-k -----]

ABOVE LEFT: VIEW OF AQUATIC GARDEN FROM INTERIOR STAIR

ABOVE: AQUATIC GARDEN BETWEEN OFFICE BUILDINGS

AQUATIC GARDEN

YELLOW POCKET GARDEN

WHITE POCKET GARDEN

Kathryn Gustafson
GUSTAFSON GUTHRIE NICHOL LTD.
Seattle, Washington
with **Piet Oudolf**, Hummelo, the Netherlands,
and **Robert Israel**, Los Angeles, California

LURIE GARDEN Millennium Park

Chicago, Illinois 2000–04

Lurie Garden is a three-acre area set within downtown Chicago's new lakefront Millennium Park, which is entirely constructed on a concrete slab covering an underground parking garage and railroad tracks. Landscape architect Kathryn Gustafson creates a subtle and sensuous garden with surrounding topiary walls and undulating landforms. The sculptural topography of this extraordinarily colorful site has its own distinct identity despite proximity to Frank O. Gehry & Associates' exuberant Pritzker Pavilion band shell and monumental sculptures by contemporary artists. Gustafson's design—developed with Dutch plantsman Piet Oudolf and the Los Angeles–based theatrical designer Robert Israel—responds to the desire for a relatively quiet, contemplative space but also the need to accommodate large crowds as they enter and exit the adjacent band shell area and move through the garden to the street and garage entrances.

Unlike a traditional walled park or garden, where one might expect to find an open center (such as lawn or paving) surrounded by a colorful planted border, the center of Lurie Garden is divided into two principal zones that the designers call the "light plate" and the "dark plate," in reference to sun and shade respectively. Narrow paths cut through the broad raised beds of the light section, densely planted with perennials in a four-foot-thick layer of soil. The grade change of the raised beds suggests the gentle hill-and-dale landscape of the Midwest prairie. Oudolf specified the plants for color, form, structure, and seasonal change. Broad swaths ranging from pinks to blues to golden tones of dried grasses in winter define this zone. Limestone, concrete, and gravel paths are consonant with the theme. The dark section, with its grove of cherry and redbud trees and an understory of perennials and shrubs, gives one a sense of shelter and shade. Underfoot, dark Chinese granite paving emphasizes the chromatic shift.

Separating the two zones are a boardwalk, water channel, and pool, which the designers refer to as the "seam." These elements cut an arc through the garden, tracing an old retaining wall that protected the city from the lake, reminding one that the entire park occupies a century-old artificial landfill. A fifteen-foot-high hedge defines the garden's perimeter walls. Popularly referred to as the "shoulder hedge," its muscular contours appear to support Gehry's crowning band shell in the distance when viewed from the garden. A permanent metal armature prefigures the desired silhouette of the hedge and will serve as a pruning guide for the plants—a mix of evergreen and deciduous shrubs. The sculpted profile is a contemporary riff on traditional topiary. Openings cut within this verdant wall lead to paths that thread through the garden's interior, allowing one to explore the various moods created by the diverse spaces.

—PR

AERIAL VIEW LOOKING WEST TOWARD THE
MILLENNIUM PARK SITE BEFORE CONSTRUCTION

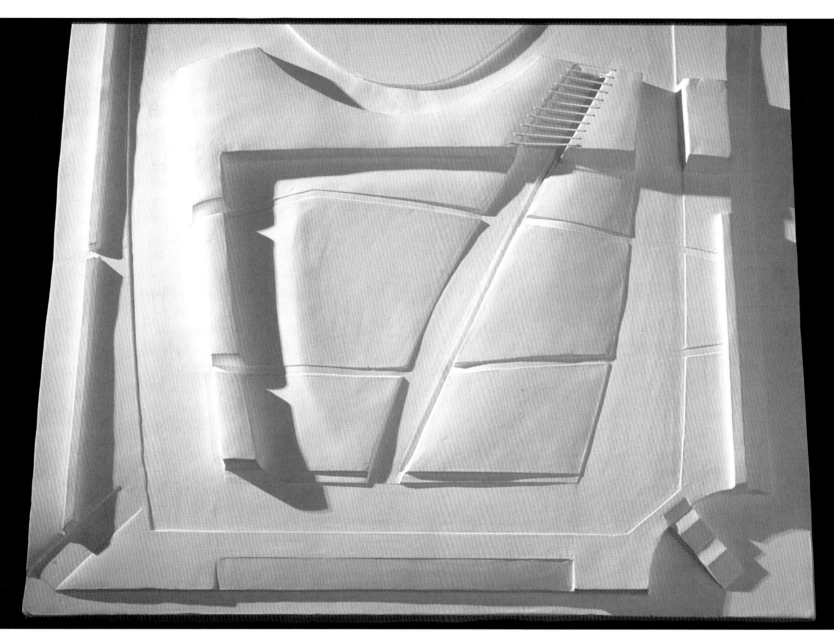

CONCEPT MODEL, VIEW FROM ABOVE

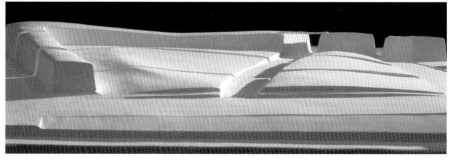

CONCEPT MODEL, VIEW LOOKING NORTH

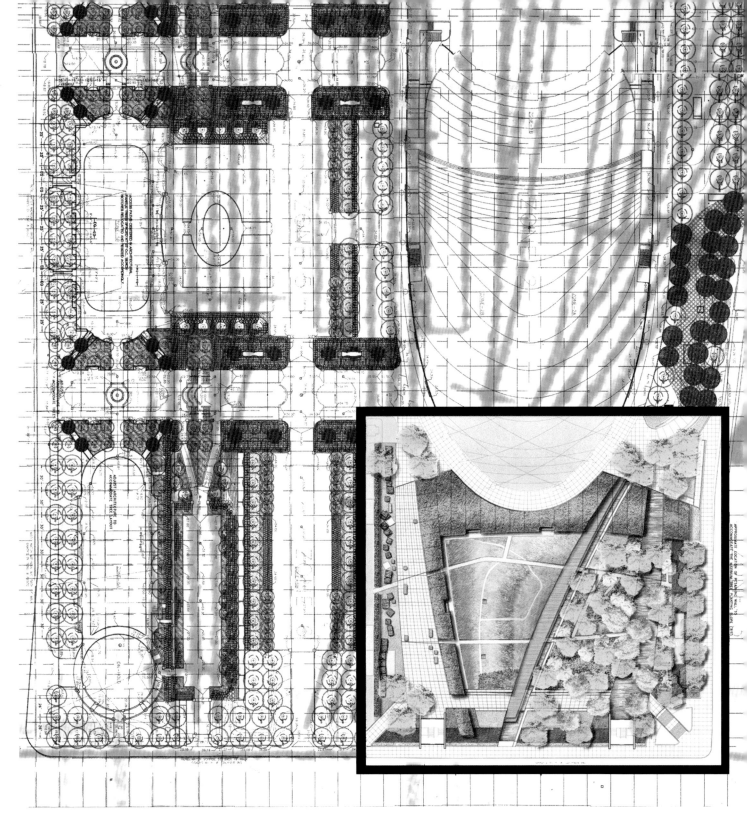

SITE PLAN OF LURIE GARDEN IN MILLENNIUM PARK, SPRING

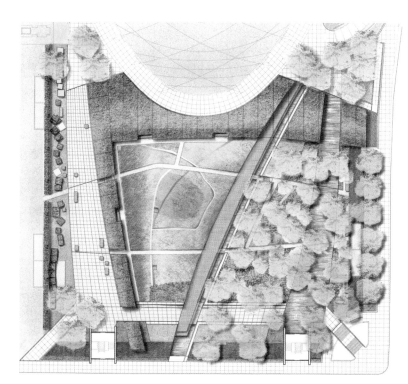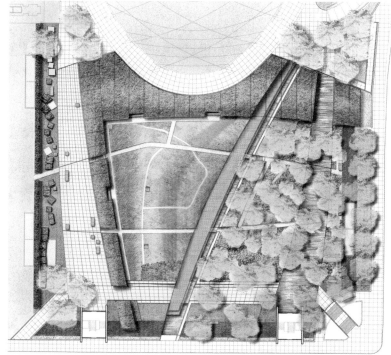

PLAN OF GARDEN, SUMMER AND AUTUMN (LEFT) AND WINTER (RIGHT)

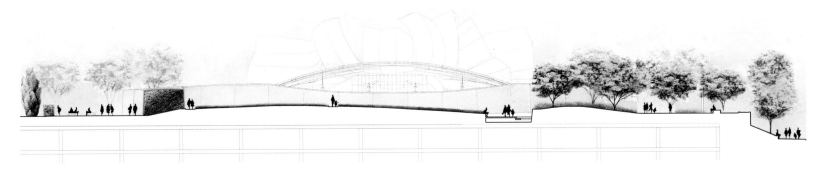

TOP: VIEW OF GARDEN LOOKING NORTH TOWARD HEDGE
AND PRITZKER PAVILION

ABOVE: EAST-WEST SECTION LOOKING NORTH

VIEW OF BOARDWALK, LOOKING NORTH

TOP: VIEW OF POOL AND BOARDWALK LOOKING NORTH TOWARD
PRITZKER PAVILION

ABOVE: VIEW OF GARDEN'S INTERIOR LOOKING EAST

Farshid Moussavi and
Alejandro Zaera-Polo
FOREIGN OFFICE ARCHITECTS
London, England

SOUTHEAST COASTAL PARK Forum 2004
Barcelona, Spain 2000–04

Foreign Office Architects has sculpted a new topography for Barcelona's Southeast Coastal Park. Situated on twelve and a half acres of landfill, the park was constructed as part of UNESCO's Forum 2004 (see also pp. 144–47). In addition to a waterfront leisure area with access to the sea, the competition program specified that plans include two auditoriums, one with seven thousand seats and one with two thousand. Inspired by the ability of dunes to withstand harsh sea wind and protect flora and fauna, the designers rigorously analyzed their formation. They also analyzed sight lines and acoustics for various stage configurations and seating arrangements in order to generate the shape of the auditoriums. Rather than begin with a preconceived plan, the architects allowed their research to determine the site's layout.

Undulating forms traverse the site. Like naturally occurring berms, the park crests and slopes parallel to the coastline. The site abuts a two-story parking garage and negotiates a forty-foot change in elevation from the roof of the garage to the sea. An esplanade runs along the ridgeline. As the dunes descend, the esplanade breaks into several circulation paths that zigzag down to sea level. As the paths bifurcate, program elements are inserted. Located at opposite ends, two swales form the auditoriums. Seating is built into the slope, accentuating the artificial topography. Behind the stage, a second berm rises to form a storage area for the theaters.

The inland side of the dune is completely planted with grasses, reeds, and trees—all characteristic of natural dunes. Facing the sea, customized paving stones in three different colors follow the contours of the site. Their crescent shape allows them to adjust to the varying slope conditions without requiring cutting, and the rounded edges mean that grass can grow between them. Laid in rows of alternating color, the pavers create strong graphic striations that draw the visitor's attention back to the ground plane. This crescent shape, reminiscent of the designers' analysis of acoustics and sight lines, is also evocative of parabolic dunes, the park's genius loci.

—IS

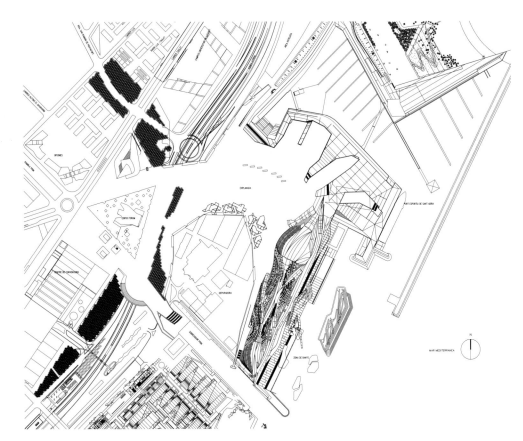

SITE PLAN

AERIAL VIEW DURING CONSTRUCTION

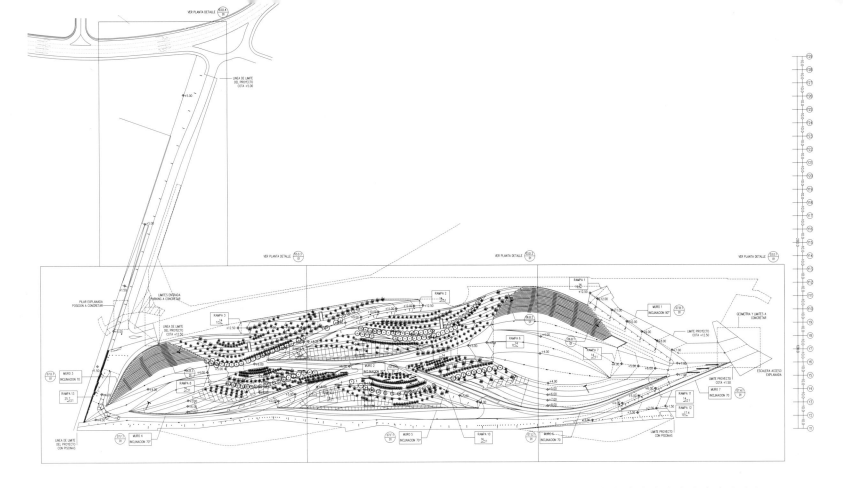

PLANTING PLAN

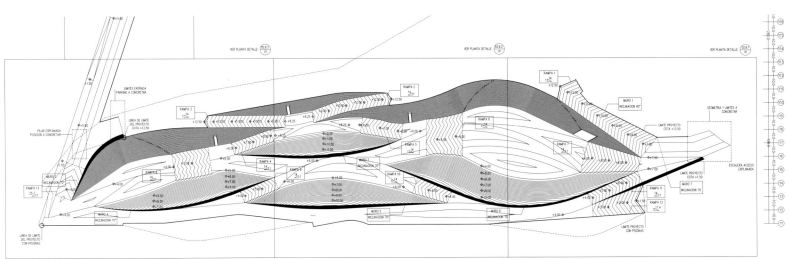

PLANTA GENERAL DEFINICION TOPOGRAFICA
CURVAS DE NIVEL A 200 mm

TOPOGRAPHIC PLAN

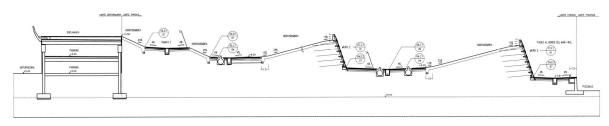

01 SECCION A-A

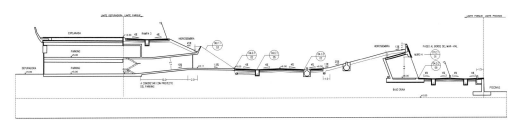

02 SECCION B-B

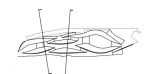

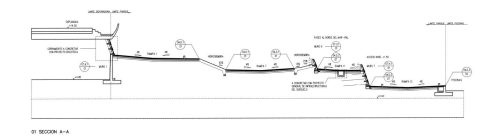

01 SECCION A-A

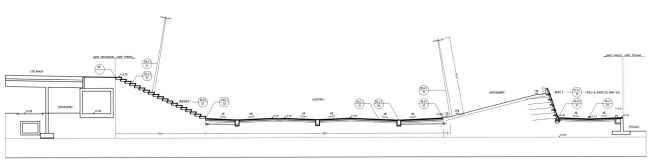

02 SECCION B-B

SECTIONS

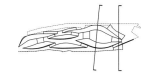

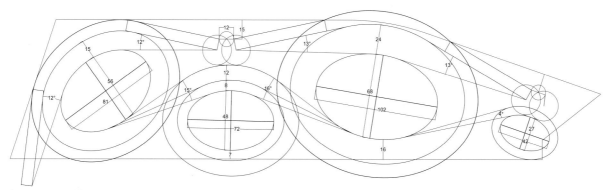

Geometry rules proliferation over the site

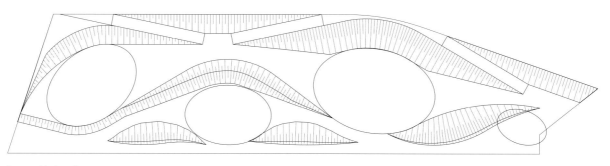

Topographical result

GEOMETRIC CONFIGURATION OF SITE (TOP); RESULTING TOPOGRAPHY (BOTTOM)

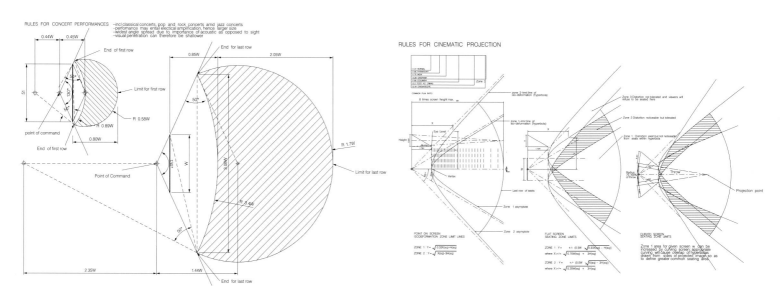

ANALYTIC DRAWING FOR CONCERT PERFORMANCES

ANALYTIC DRAWING FOR CINEMA PROJECTIONS

AERIAL VIEW FROM NORTH DURING CONSTRUCTION

AERIAL VIEW FROM SOUTH DURING CONSTRUCTION

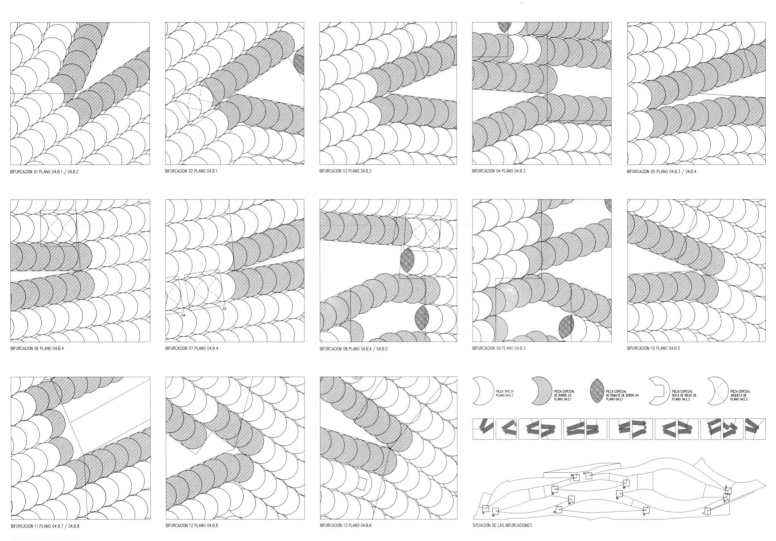

BIFURCACION 01 PLANO 04.B.1 / 04.B.2

BIFURCACION 02 PLANO 04.B.1

BIFURCACION 03 PLANO 04.B.3

BIFURCACION 04 PLANO 04.B.3

BIFURCACION 05 PLANO 04.B.3 / 04.B.4

BIFURCACION 06 PLANO 04.B.4

BIFURCACION 07 PLANO 04.B.4

BIFURCACION 08 PLANO 04.B.4 / 04.B.5

BIFURCACION 09 PLANO 04.B.5

BIFURCACION 10 PLANO 04.B.5

BIFURCACION 11 PLANO 04.B.7 / 04.B.8

BIFURCACION 12 PLANO 04.B.8

BIFURCACION 13 PLANO 04.B.8

SITUACION DE LAS BIFURCACIONES

PIEZA TIPO 01
PLANO 04.E.1

PIEZA ESPECIAL
DE BORDE 03
PLANO 04.E.1

PIEZA ESPECIAL
DE REMATE DE BORDE 04
PLANO 04.E.1

PIEZA ESPECIAL
BOCA DE RIEGO 06
PLANO 04.E.2

PIEZA ESPECIAL
ARQUETA 08
PLANO 04.E.2

PAVING SYSTEM

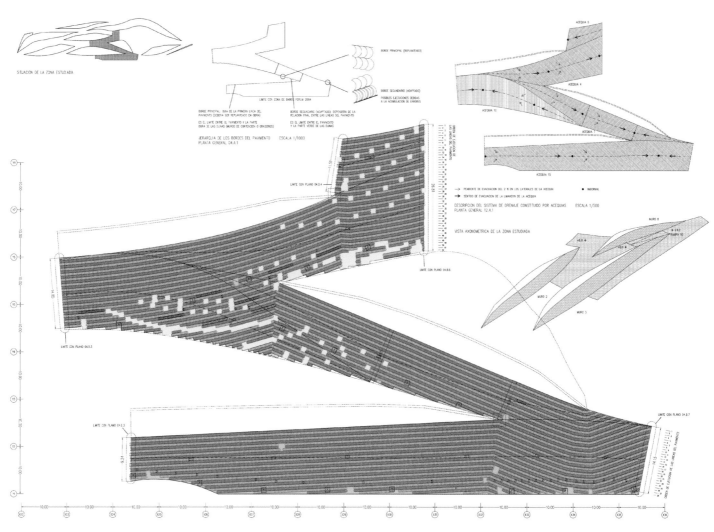

SITUACION DE LA ZONA ESTUDIADA

DETAIL OF PAVING PLAN

ENRIC MIRALLES and **CARME PINÓS**
Barcelona, Spain

IGUALADA CEMETERY PARK

Igualada, Spain 1985–96 (partially complete)

Despite its proximity to the town's industrial outskirts, Igualada Cemetery Park is astonishingly tranquil. Its unlikely setting—a secluded, semiarid river valley whose friable walls have been shaped and cut over time by the Riera de Odena that flows through it—suggested few practical uses and may have inspired Enric Miralles to poetically describe the project as a relationship between the landscape and the forgotten.

The design is predicated on excavation as much as construction. The principal open space is a wide, plaza-like path that descends from the entrance gate toward the riverbed. This path is lined with inward and outward sloping walls and broad sheltering eaves that echo the surrounding topographical formations carved by the river over thousands of years. Crypts are integrated into the walls. An upper-level terrace, also lined with crypts, adds to the spatial complexity of the site and imparts a sense of sculpting of the land. Stone from the location, small prefabricated units of concrete made on-site for the walls, Cor-Ten steel, and rough-hewn weathered railroad ties laid in the path in a seemingly random pattern harmonize with the region's rugged terrain.

The excavated path, lined in stone aggregate, culminates in a cul-de-sac surrounded by burial tombs. Once completed, it will descend in a zigzag pattern across the site to the river below. Densely planted trees provide shade and a feeling of life and renewal. Loose stone held together in gabion walls and prefabricated concrete screens also create a dramatic play between light and shadow while allowing vegetation such as thyme, rosemary, and dozens of varieties of wildflowers to grow in a natural and uncultivated manner in crevices and atop the landforms.

In this serene environment of humble materials visitors are transported from everyday concerns as they make their gentle descent and ascent. Miralles and Carme Pinós intended the open space sheltered by the flanking sloped walls to cause one to "lose all frames of reference except for the sunlight of the interior." The juxtaposition of the park's constructed forms and open spaces with the geologic strata of the surrounding natural landscape reinforces one's awareness of time and memory.

—PR

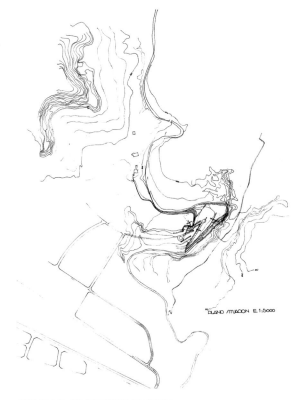

SITE PLAN, COMPETITION DRAWING

TOP AND ABOVE: ENTRANCE WITH OPEN GATE

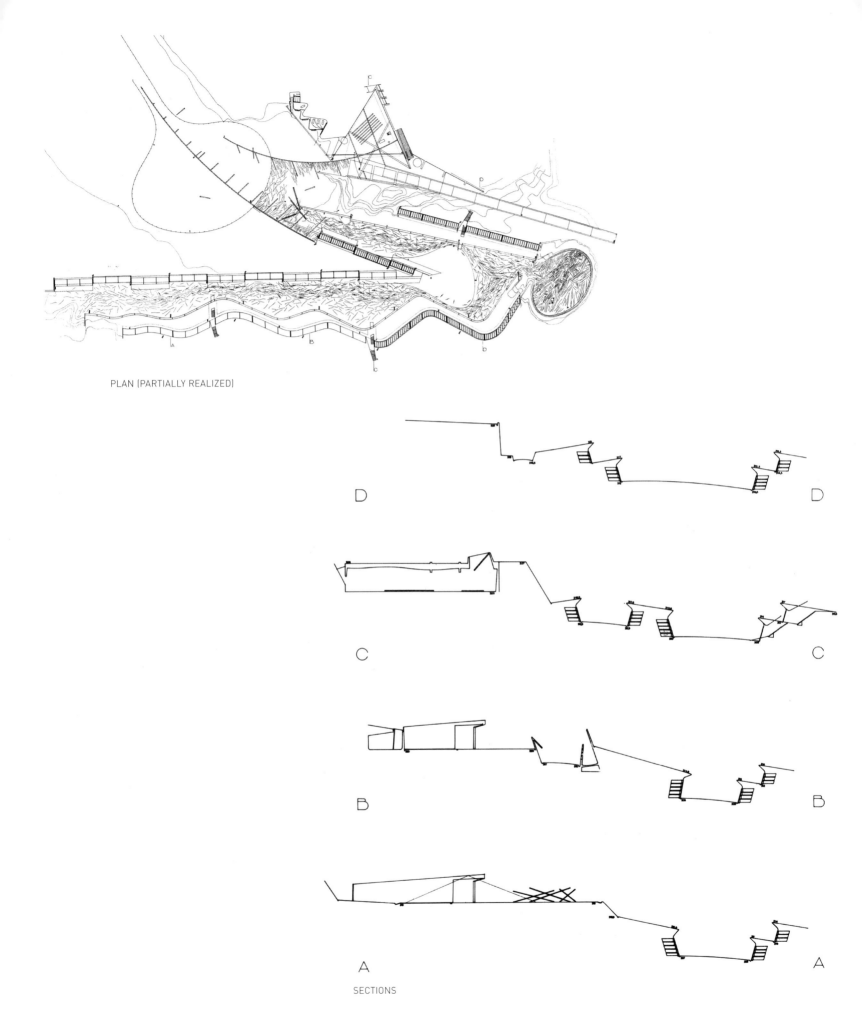

PLAN (PARTIALLY REALIZED)

D   D

C   C

B   B

A   A

SECTIONS

PATH WITH CRYPTS AND INLAID RAILROAD TIES

TOP: VIEW FROM UPPER-LEVEL CRYPT TERRACE

ABOVE: VIEW TOWARD BURIAL TOMBS WITH
UPPER AND LOWER CRYPTS ON LEFT

ABOVE: BURIAL TOMBS WITH GABION WALLS

ABOVE RIGHT: VIEW FROM UPPER-LEVEL
TERRACE TOWARD PATH

VIEW FROM UPPER-LEVEL TERRACE TOWARD
PATH AND CRYPT

WEISS/MANFREDI ARCHITECTS
New York, New York

OLYMPIC SCULPTURE PARK Seattle Art Museum

Seattle, Washington 2001–06

The degraded site of a former fuel storage and transfer station is being transformed into the new eight-and-a-half-acre Olympic Sculpture Park on Elliott Bay in downtown Seattle. A forty-foot grade change from street to sea level meant that the steeply sloping site required extensive excavation and remediation. Further complicating the site, the four-lane Elliott Avenue and the tracks of the Burlington Northern Santa Fe Railroad divide the site into three parcels. These complex conditions invited a bold design of new landforms to create a unified space that responds as much to the new and existing infrastructure as to the Seattle Art Museum's public and artistic program. The park's design reshapes existing ground and constructs a new topography to create connections where none previously existed.

A 2,200-foot zigzag path bridging the existing transportation systems defines Weiss/Manfredi Architects' design for a continuous landform that links the three disparate parcels. This path leads visitors from a new concrete, steel, and glass pavilion (for art, performances, educational programs, a café, and underground parking) at the upper edge of the site through a variety of outdoor sculpture galleries and concludes at the shoreline. The steepest slopes of this artificial topography are formed by mechanically stabilized earth clad with overlapping precast concrete panels, while steel and cast-in-place concrete support the bridges. As one traverses the crushed stone path, views are directed north toward the sea and mountains and then shift south toward the city and port. Beneath this constructed surface an infrastructural backbone will connect lights, teledata ports, water lines, and power to support multimedia artwork and changing exhibitions.

As a setting for art, the park is designed to accommodate temporary installations, performance art, works by artists from the museum's permanent collection (Alexander Calder, Richard Serra, Tony Smith, Mark di Suvero, and others) and commissions by contemporary artists (including Mark Dion, Louise Bourgeois, and Teresita Fernandez), a seating project by Roy McMakin, and both indoor and outdoor video projects. The planting plan, developed with landscape architect Charles Anderson, calls for three archetypal landscapes of the Northwest. The most sheltered area of the park, a dense evergreen forest valley with an understory of ferns and ground cover, will connect to the pavilion with ascending grass terraces. A deciduous forest of aspen trees will dramatically mark seasonal changes. Finally, a restored shoreline and new beach will replace a seawall and aid in the restoration of the coastline's marine ecology.

The landscapes of this new urban park are designed to impart spatial, color, and textural variety while framing views of art, the city, and the dramatic background of Puget Sound and the Olympic Mountains. The design not only brings sculpture outside the museum walls but also brings a new experience of nature to the city.

—PR

CONCEPTUAL STUDY OF SITE DESIGN

AERIAL VIEW OF SITE CONDITIONS BEFORE CONSTRUCTION

RENDERING OF VIEW TOWARD DOWNTOWN SEATTLE

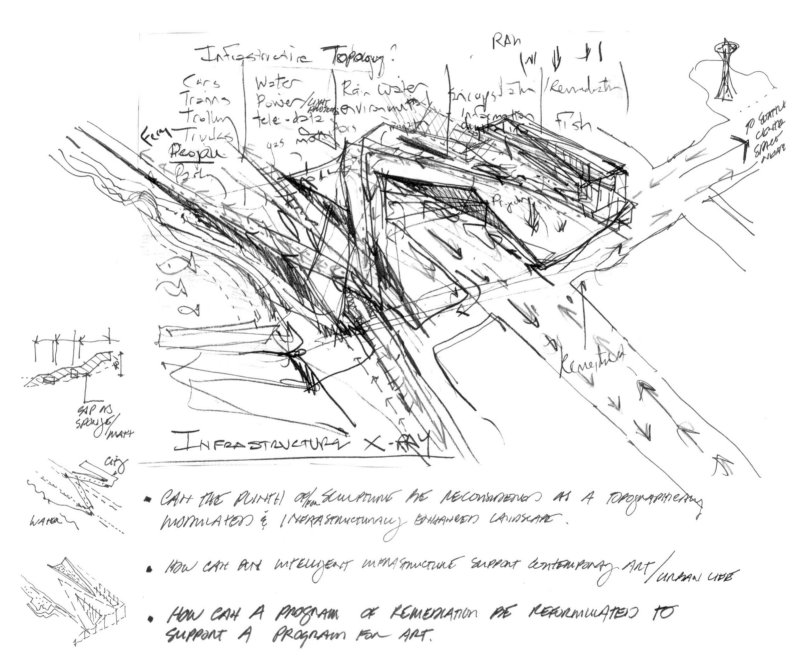

INFRASTRUCTURE X-RAY

- CAN THE PLINTH OF/FOR SCULPTURE BE RECONSIDERED AS A TOPOGRAPHICALLY MODULATED & INFRASTRUCTURALLY ENHANCED LANDSCAPE.

- HOW CAN AN INTELLIGENT INFRASTRUCTURE SUPPORT CONTEMPORARY ART/URBAN LIFE

- HOW CAN A PROGRAM OF REMEDIATION BE REFORMULATED TO SUPPORT A PROGRAM FOR ART.

ANNOTATED STUDY OF INFRASTRUCTURE

RENDERING OF AERIAL VIEW TOWARD ELLIOTT BAY
AND OLYMPIC MOUNTAINS

TOP: RENDERING OF PLATFORM OVER RAILROAD

ABOVE: RENDERING OF VIEW FROM AUTOMOBILE OF
ELLIOTT AVENUE OVERPASS AND VIDEO PROJECTIONS

RENDERING OF PARK PAVILION FROM
BROAD STREET

RENDERING OF NIGHT VIEW FROM ELLIOTT BAY

RENDERING OF SCULPTURE GARDEN AND
PARK PAVILION

RENDERING OF VIEW FROM GROVE TOWARD PARK PAVILION

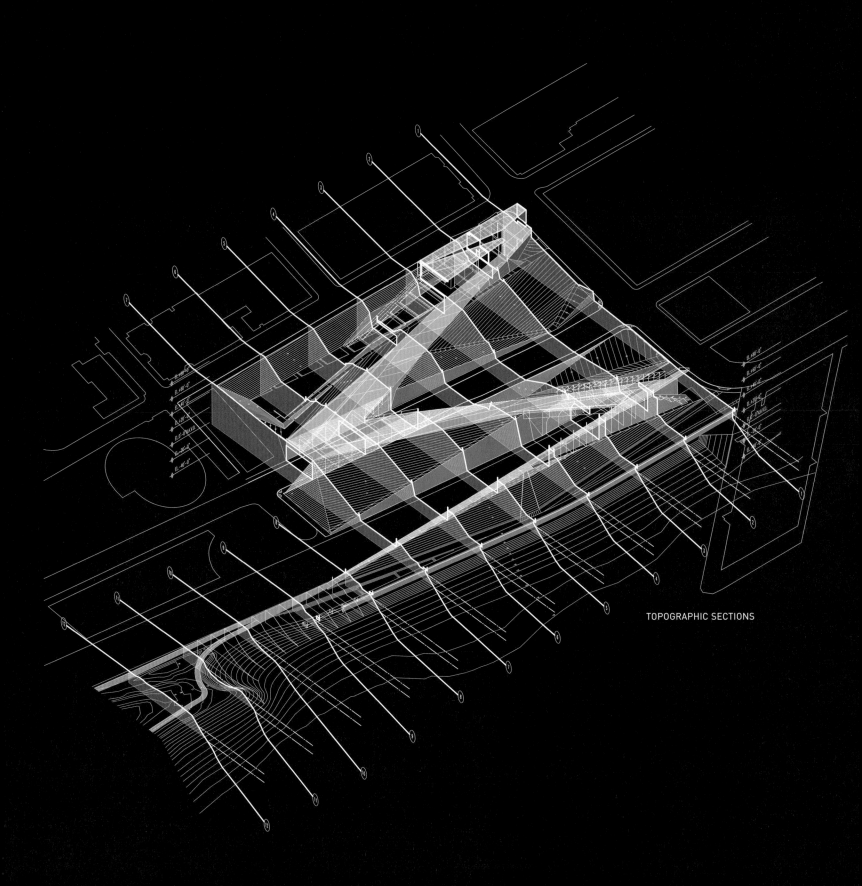

TOPOGRAPHIC SECTIONS

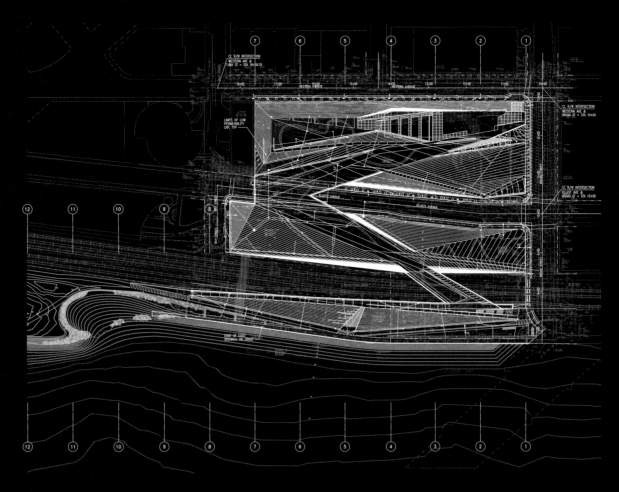

CONTOUR PLAN

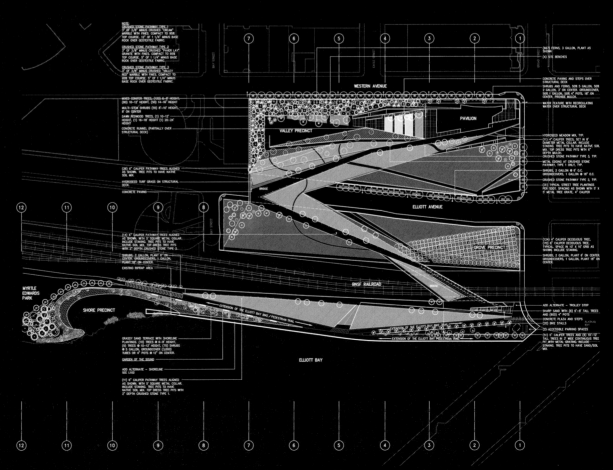

LANDSCAPE PLANTING PLAN

Peter Latz
LATZ + PARTNER
Kranzberg, Germany

DUISBURG-NORD LANDSCAPE PARK International Building Exhibition (IBA) Emscher Park

Duisburg, Germany 1990–2002

The towering blast furnace of the former Thyssen Steelworks is an unlikely beacon to signal a new park of some 570 acres amid the densely populated Ruhr district in western Germany. Existing engine houses, mill buildings, bridges, gas tanks, empty coke and ore bunkers, and traces of rail lines are incorporated into the park as awesome monumental sculptures and landforms to serve new programmatic activities and as reminders of the site's history. Rather than try to erase the past, which was fiscally irresponsible if not impossible, Peter Latz recognized that the combination of industry and nature results in an experience rich with memories, associations, and feelings. The project has expanded the idea of what a park can be, and set new standards for similar environmental, economic, and social transformations happening around the region.

Latz's general concept plan takes its cue from the existing infrastructure: the network of rail lines that gives coherence to the system of paths (such as the distinctive bermed rail harp that fans out across the site), steel catwalks, a canal, and monumental bunkers, all of which are transformed from their previous practical uses into landscape features. New paths and elevated footbridges combined with the old allow one to experience the site from varying levels. Pedestrian and bike paths thread through the prairie-like site and connect newly created plazas, gardens, and recreational areas. From above, new pedestrian bridges, echoing the old infrastructure, offer a commanding vantage from which to absorb the panorama and to look down on the grid of ore and sintering bunkers, now transformed by recreational programs such as children's playgrounds, rock climbing clubs, and meditative, enclosed gardens.

On this vast site, plant life provides another structuring element. Some areas are clearly planted, such as the grove of flowering cherry trees, landscaped gardens in and around the old sintering bunkers, and community gardens. The generally poor soil quality of the majority of the site, however, limits what species will grow. Birch and poplar trees, raspberries, and over two hundred species of native and exotic wildflowers, grasses, and lichens are among the pioneer plants, which over time will improve the soil and allow other species to take root. The canal is another key element in Latz's concept for the park. Formerly a contaminated sewage channel (which has been resealed and relocated further underground), the system of water retention pools together with the canal provides aesthetic pleasure and symbolizes this brownfield's environmental remediation.

—PR

TOP: BLAST FURNACE LIGHTING INSTALLATION
DESIGNED BY JONATHAN PARK

LEFT: AERIAL VIEW OF THYSSEN STEELWORKS' DUISBURG
MEIDERICH IRON MILL, UNDATED PHOTOGRAPH

OPPOSITE: PLAZA WITH CHERRY TREES ADJACENT TO
COWPER STOVES AND BLAST FURNACE

AERIAL VIEW OF RAIL HARP

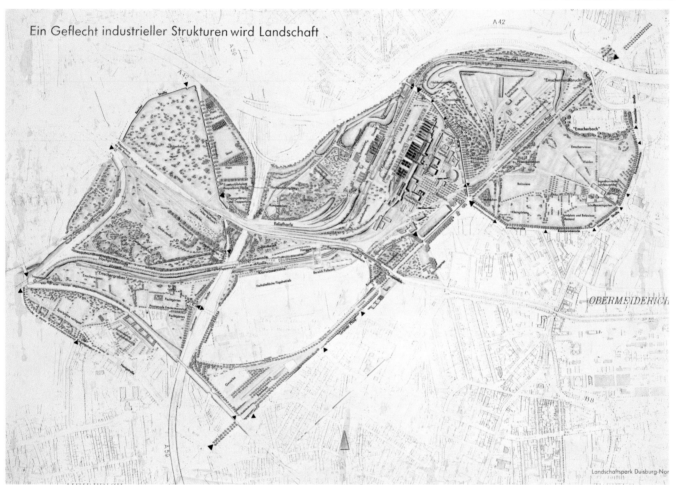

Ein Geflecht industrieller Strukturen wird Landschaft

SITE PLAN

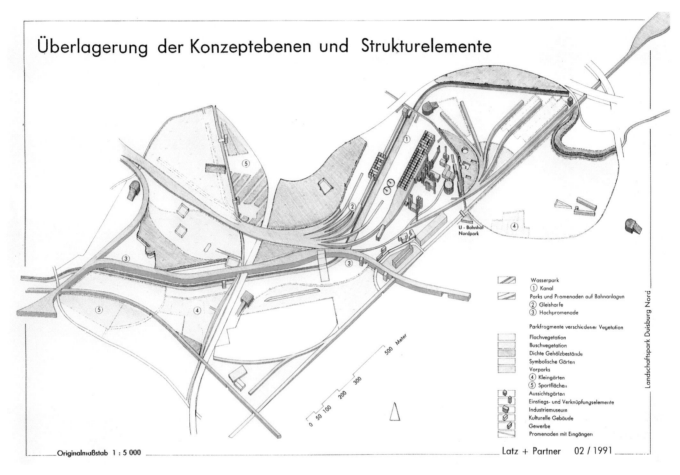

Überlagerung der Konzeptebenen und Strukturelemente

CONCEPTUAL PLAN AND PRINCIPAL STRUCTURAL ELEMENTS, INCLUDING WATER PARK, RAIL HARP AND
ELEVATED WALKWAYS, VARIOUS VEGETATION ZONES, COMMUNITY GARDENS AND SPORTS FIELDS, AND BUILDINGS

AERIAL VIEW OF ORE BUNKERS

PIAZZA METALLICA

PATH CUT THROUGH ORE BUNKER WALLS

PLAYGROUND IN ORE BUNKERS

ORE BUNKER ADAPTED FOR ROCK CLIMBING WALLS

FAR LEFT: CANAL AND RAIL CRANE

LEFT: SCUBA DIVER IN WATER COOLING POOL

VIEW FROM SLAG HEAP OF SINTERING BUNKERS, NEW PEDESTRIAN BRIDGE, AND RAIL CRANE

WATER RETENTION POOL

LEFT: SINTERING BUNKERS

ABOVE LEFT: SINTERING BUNKER GARDEN

ABOVE: SALVIA GARDEN AND CHIMNEY RUIN

LEFT: RUINS WITH PIONEER PLANTS

HARGREAVES ASSOCIATES
San Francisco, California
Cambridge, Massachusetts

CRISSY FIELD Presidio National Park
San Francisco, California 1994–2001

The transformation of Crissy Field, an early-twentieth-century U.S. Army airstrip, into a one-hundred-acre urban public park was an exercise in restraint for lead designer George Hargreaves. The site's vast scale and its spectacular setting on the northern edge of Presidio National Park along San Francisco Bay—with magnificent panoramas of the Golden Gate Bridge and distant hills—prompted Hargreaves to design in several broad strokes. Six major zones now define Crissy Field: the rehabilitation of a 1920s-era grassed airfield; a mile-long promenade for walkers, joggers, and bikers; newly restored tidal wetlands; beach and dunes; and two activity areas at either end of the park—West Bluff, a picnic area, and East Beach, a large gathering space and planted parking area that can accommodate the huge number of avid windsurfers who come for the bay's steady gusting winds.

The majority of the site had been previously paved. To create the new park, 87,000 tons of hazardous materials were removed and seventy acres of asphalt and concrete were pulled up, crushed, and recycled for use beneath pathways and as base support for new parking lots. The tidal wetlands, newly designed by Hargreaves, recall the natural condition that existed on the site nearly a century earlier, before the army appropriated them as a dump and landfill. After restoring the wetlands and their important biological functions, the resulting excavated earth was recycled and spread on the airfield, giving this new grassy expanse greater height and definition along its bermed edges. In the wetlands and dunes new plantings of flowering native species with gray-green and silvery foliage are chromatically distinct from the bright green grass that covers much of the site.

The promenade, with its simple, arcing gesture, creates a strong geometric form that defines the site's linear structure. Its gentle curve echoes the coastline and connects the different areas of the park while allowing one to enjoy the breathtaking views. This linear geometry is also reflected in other elements of the design, such as the long benches and the parallel rows of subtle landforms in the picnic area. These grassy ridges add playful visual interest and also serve a practical function as windbreaks.

—PR

AERIAL VIEW OF CONDITIONS BEFORE CONSTRUCTION

AERIAL VIEW AFTER CONSTRUCTION

134

ABOVE: SHORELINE BEFORE RESTORATION

RIGHT: SHORELINE AFTER RESTORATION

ABOVE: WETLANDS AREA BEFORE RESTORATION

RIGHT: TIDAL WETLANDS AFTER RESTORATION

ABOVE: ASPHALT RUNWAY BEFORE RESTORATION

RIGHT: GRASS AIRFIELD AND TIDAL WETLANDS AFTER RESTORATION

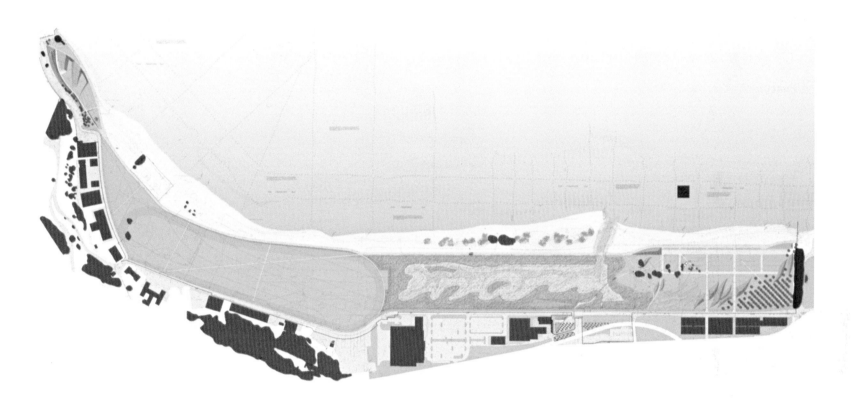

SITE PLAN

VIEW TOWARD DOWNTOWN SAN FRANCISCO FROM PRESIDIO OVERLOOK
SHOWING AIRFIELD, TIDAL WETLANDS, AND PROMENADE

FAR LEFT: WEST BLUFF PICNIC AREA

LEFT: KITE FLYING ON AIRFIELD

VIEW OF TIDAL WETLANDS AND GOLDEN GATE BRIDGE

AERIAL VIEW OF LANDFORMS, GROVE, AND
PLANTED PARKING AREA AT EAST BEACH

ABOVE: PICNIC AREA LANDFORM ALONG
PROMENADE

LEFT: PLANTED PARKING AREA AND PROME-
NADE AT EAST BEACH

MICHEL and **CLAIRE CORAJOUD**
Paris, France

ADR and **GEORGES DESCOMBES**
Geneva, Switzerland

PARC DE LA COUR DU MAROC

Paris, France 2003; projected completion, 2006

A ten-acre site in the heart of Paris's densely populated eighteenth arrondissement is being transformed from an abandoned zone of warehouses and railway tracks into a vibrant urban park named for the adjacent Rue du Maroc. The narrow site, approximately 330 by 1,500 feet, is hemmed in on three sides by streets and borders an active rail yard.

The landscape architects' vision of transforming a working landscape into a place of leisure activities was inspired by traces of the former railroad. One of their principal objectives was to preserve a sense of linearity and to create a simplicity and harmony across the long, parallel bands that delineate program and activity zones. While the design honors the rational and functional layout of the tracks that once defined the site, subtle changes in the ground plane, variety in paths and materials, a rich and diverse planting palette, and recreational activities add complexity to the plan.

The main entrance is located midway along the Rue d'Auberville. To the right a bamboo garden borders the street and from there paths and terraced gardens zigzag upward to an elevated recreation deck. Planting beds, flowering trees and perennials, and trough-like pools enliven the garden's path. The raised deck is deliberately sited adjacent to the active railroad tracks in part to serve as a visual and sound buffer between the trains and the quieter areas of the park. Underneath the deck is ample storage space for park equipment.

Left of the main entrance is the esplanade, the only area intended to be active twenty-four hours a day. Benches, a kiosk for refreshments, trees, and fine gravel paving recall the materials and activities associated with traditional Parisian parks. Behind the esplanade a boardwalk with long tables provides a place for groups to gather for picnics. A water canal with aquatic plants divides the boardwalk from a gravel garden. This garden—a reference to the ballast of the abandoned railroad tracks—is intentionally unrefined and meant to appeal as much to adventurous kids as to horticultural enthusiasts: with input from a plant specialist, the designers have specified a wide variety of hardy wildflowers that will thrive with minimal care, in part a financial consideration. Behind the gravel garden is another linear band—a green meadow. Abutting the meadow is a paved plaza with fountains. Broad steps, doubling as an amphitheatre, lead to a bosque of trees and the raised sports deck.

The adjacent rail yard is revealed in places. A steel footbridge elevated sixteen feet off the ground borders the tracks and connects the park to the level of the raised side streets and recreation deck. The change in level also offers variety to the path and vistas of the park, the railroad, and the white dome of Sacré-Coeur, the nearby Parisian landmark.

—PR

TOP: VIEW TOWARD ADJACENT RAILROAD AND SACRÉ-COEUR BEFORE CONSTRUCTION

ABOVE: VIEW FROM SOUTH BEFORE CONSTRUCTION

COMPETITION MODEL, VIEW FROM SOUTH

1. EAST-WEST CROSS SECTION THROUGH
MEADOW AND ESPLANADE LOOKING NORTH

2. EAST-WEST CROSS SECTION THROUGH
TERRACES LOOKING NORTH

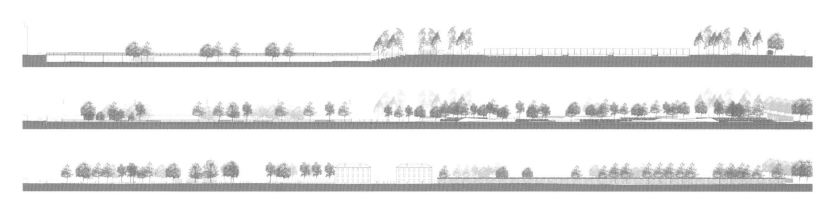

3.–5. NORTH-SOUTH SECTIONS LOOKING WEST SHOWING
PRINCIPAL GARDENS AND CHANGES IN GROUND LEVEL

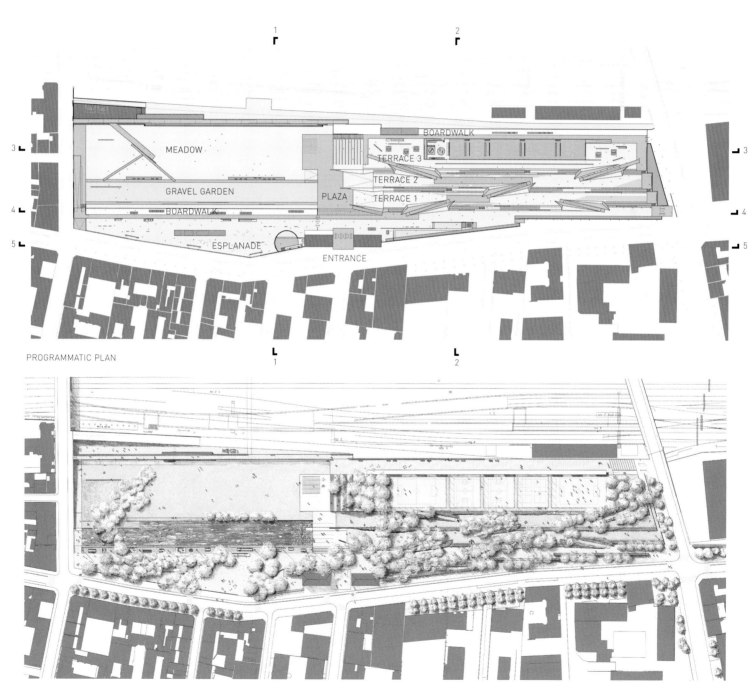

1

2

3   3

4   4

5   5

MEADOW

BOARDWALK

TERRACE 3

TERRACE 2

GRAVEL GARDEN

PLAZA   TERRACE 1

BOARDWALK

ESPLANADE

ENTRANCE

PROGRAMMATIC PLAN

1   2

SITE PLAN

RENDERING OF FOUNTAIN AREA

RENDERING OF TERRACES

ABALOS & HERREROS
Madrid, Spain

NORTHEAST COASTAL PARK Forum 2004
Barcelona, Spain 2000–04

Barcelona's Northeast Coastal Park, designed by Abalos & Herreros, successfully combines two unlikely elements—a municipal waste-management complex and a waterfront park and beach—innovatively integrating necessary infrastructure and public space. The park served as part of the site for the First International Forum of Cultures, organized by UNESCO to promote cultural diversity and sustainable development and staged in Barcelona in 2004 (see also pp. 102–09).

Originally cut off from the city by a ring road, the site had served as the city's major services area, where a now defunct sewage treatment plant and electrical generator were also located. To showcase sustainable urban design, the existing incinerator now powers a new waste-to-energy generator. The steam heat produced by the incinerator is used to make electricity for hot and cold water as well as heating and air-conditioning for the Forum grounds and the new Diagonal Mar mixed-use district. At the base of the incinerator is a new recycling center.

In order to rehabilitate the contaminated site, the top layer of soil needed to be removed. The area was then regraded, and landfill and recycled sand were used to extend a new coastline and artificial beach over three hundred feet into the Mediterranean Sea. Each landform serves a function. Below the west lawn is an underground parking facility for the new marina. Hidden underneath a grass cover along the ring road, the so-called Mountain houses the waste-to-energy generator. The height and physical mass of this landform also act as a noise barrier. Across the street, the hillock wrapping around the incinerator is a new recycling center. An education center provides the public an opportunity to learn about the advanced technologies that made the waterfront park possible.

Visitors enter the park from the west via a wide, paved promenade. Upon passing the Mountain and education center to the left, the visitor reaches the incinerator where the promenade opens to a panoramic view of the Mediterranean. This pathway continues to a boardwalk, where large lawns spread out to the east and west. To create an immediate sense of place, mature palm trees were planted along the promenade, lawns, and beach. A paved boardwalk mosaic by artist Albert Oehlen playfully depicts a sea of fish along the beach. Reminiscent of Josep María Jujol's mosaics for Antoni Gaudí's buildings and Park Güell, the collaboration between artist and designer continues Barcelona's strong decorative art tradition. As in his paintings, Oehlen explores the boundaries between abstraction and figuration. The artist designed the fish at such a large scale that the mosaic reads as color fields from the ground level. However, from an elevated position, such as the deck on the west lawn or the Mountain trail, the park visitor begins to perceive the artist's colorful underwater world.

—IS

SITE BEFORE CONSTRUCTION

VIEW OF MODEL FROM WEST

VIEW OF MODEL FROM SOUTH

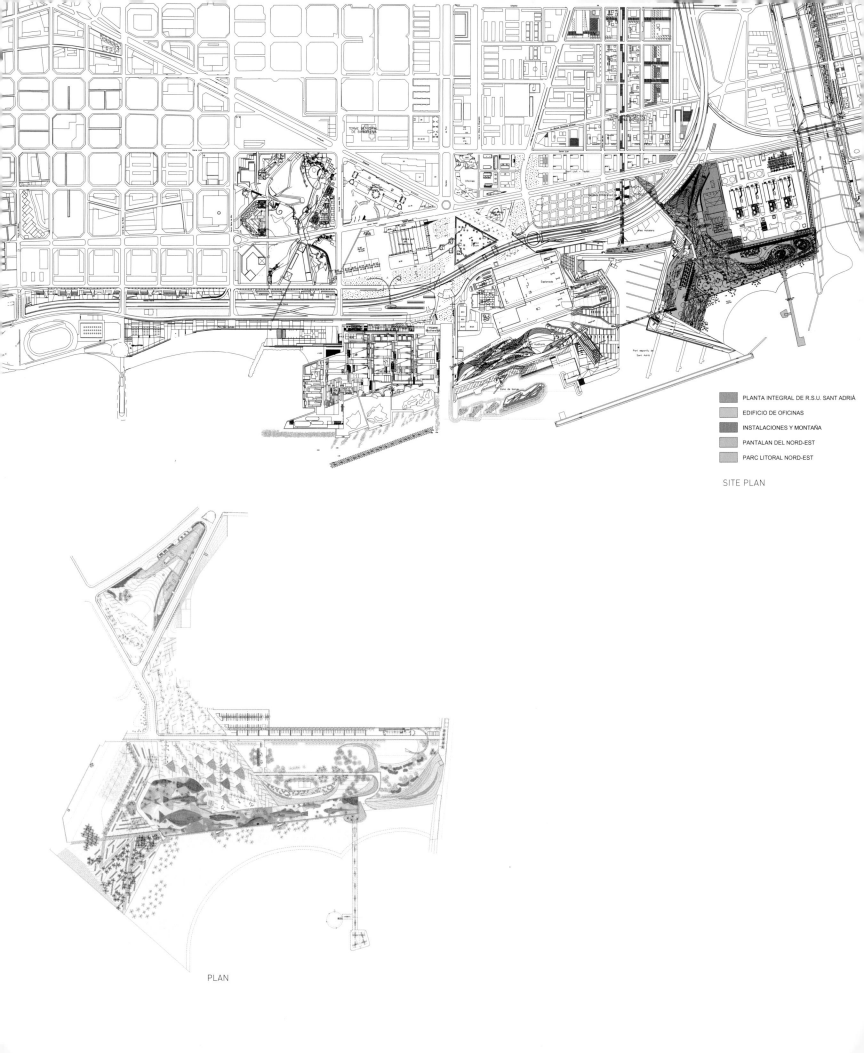

PLANTA INTEGRAL DE R.S.U. SANT ADRIÀ

EDIFICIO DE OFICINAS

INSTALACIONES Y MONTAÑA

PANTALAN DEL NORD-EST

PARC LITORAL NORD-EST

SITE PLAN

PLAN

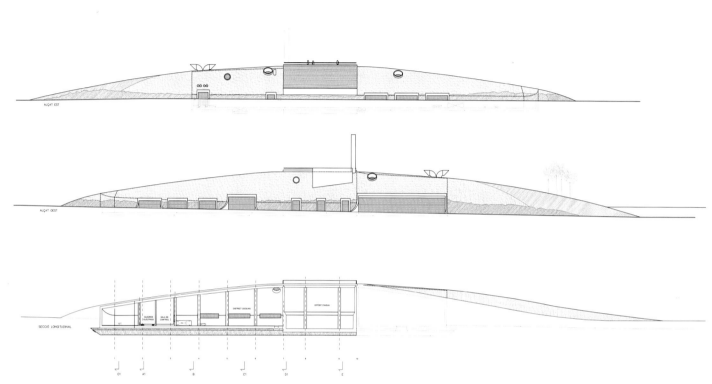

ELEVATIONS AND SECTION OF MOUNTAIN

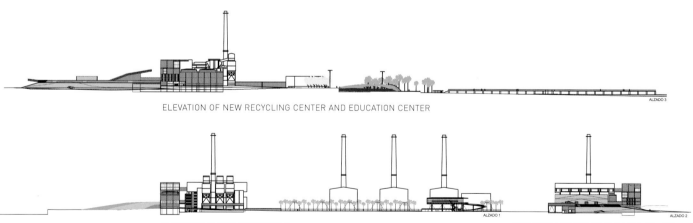

ELEVATION OF NEW RECYCLING CENTER AND EDUCATION CENTER

ELEVATION ALONG BOARDWALK

ELEVATION OF NEW RECYCLING CENTER

Michel Desvigne
DESVIGNE & DALNOKY
Paris, France

GREENWICH PENINSULA

London, England 1997–2000 (partially realized)

Greenwich Peninsula on the Thames River in London, well known for Richard Rogers Partnership's landmark Millennium Dome, was previously the site of the largest gasworks in Europe. English Partnerships acquired the contaminated three-hundred-acre area in 1997 and took on the task of its regeneration for future development. Radical decontamination measures were required, and polluted earth was removed in some places to a level of six-and-a-half feet below the existing ground, leaving a kind of tabula rasa.

Landscape architect Michel Desvigne was charged with providing a plan for the peninsula. The absence of an existing landscape with historical traces and no comprehensive development program for much of the site to succeed the millennium celebrations presented a challenge. Desvigne rejected the idea of constructing a large urban park with stereotypical features such as thematic gardens, monuments, or ponds as unfeasible, uneconomical, and premature. Rather he sought to introduce what he calls an "intermediate landscape"—to give texture and density to the formless site in a manner that is sufficiently flexible to be incorporated into future development once a program is determined. Given the scope of the site, Desvigne considered the geographical and ecological scale of an alluvial forest—a kind of Ur-landscape—that might have existed on the peninsula in another era. He drew inspiration from aerial views of mature sites, such as a poplar tree plantation in Oxfordshire, where the relationship between groves of trees and clearings is evident.

Desvigne's ambitious plan for Greenwich Peninsula was only partially realized on a portion of the site. In this initial phase, more than twelve thousand native hornbeam trees (a species better suited than poplars to the Thames site) and over one hundred thousand shrubs were densely planted, with clearings indicated for various park activities. Over time, these fast-growing trees will be thinned out and replaced by species that will grow into more mature woods, such as birch, alder, and oak, giving the project a temporal dimension. Clearings could be made according to future demands. Desvigne's work at Greenwich Peninsula also included riverfront plantings as part of the Thames Walk and an ecology park that sits on a piece of reclaimed marshland adjacent to a residential village.

A sequence of drawings, in plan and section, portrays a typical detail of Desvigne's intermediate landscape at intervals of ten, twenty-five, and fifty years. Though the new terrain is entirely constructed it appears as if nature itself had colonized the site. Desvigne's long-term approach has successfully restored a parcel of derelict land and has created a new landscape with the potential to serve as a catalyst for future development.

—PR

AERIAL VIEW OF A POPLAR TREE PLANTATION, WITNEY, OXFORDSHIRE, ENGLAND

AERIAL VIEW OF PENINSULA BEFORE
REDEVELOPMENT

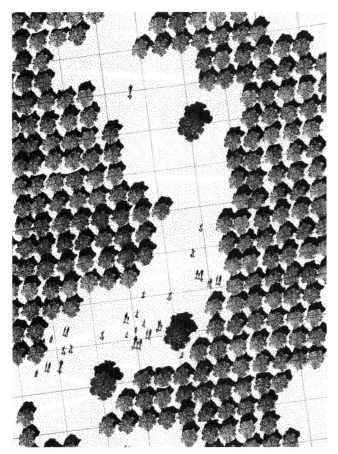

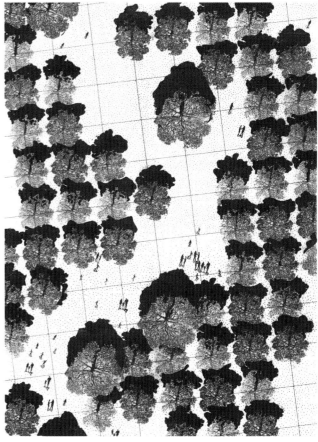

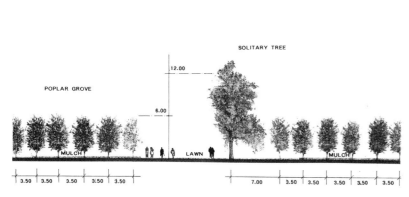

PHASE 1: YOUNG POPLAR GROVES

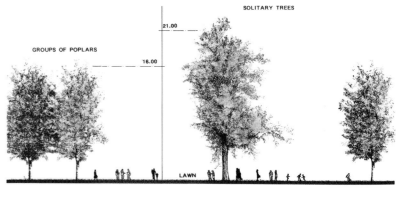

PHASE 2: POPLAR GROVES AND SOLITARY TREES AFTER TEN YEARS OF GROWTH

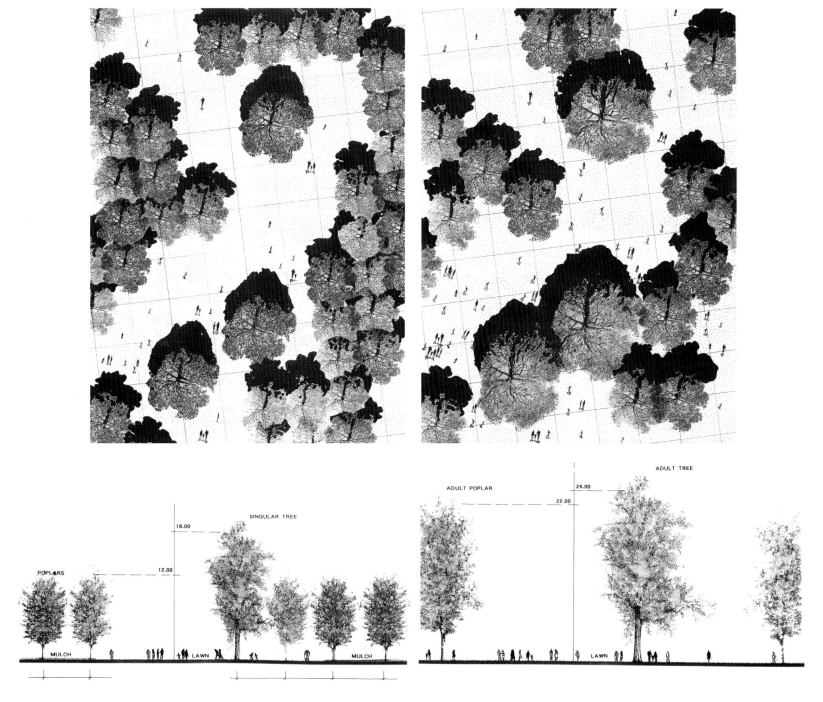

PHASE 3: GROUPS OF POPLARS AND SOLITARY TREES AFTER TWENTY-FIVE YEARS OF GROWTH

FINAL PHASE: MATURE TREES AFTER FIFTY YEARS OF GROWTH

MICHEL DESVIGNE
Paris, France

GARONNE RIVERFRONT MASTER PLAN
Bordeaux, France 2003–04; projected completion, 2034

The city of Bordeaux initially engaged Michel Desvigne to study its public spaces and to prepare a master plan that would coordinate future development in an organized and meaningful way. This exercise led to Desvigne's proposal for a new urban park along the Garonne River, which seeks to restore an industrial landscape that is ripe for transformation. The swath of land, measuring about 330 acres along a five-mile stretch of the river's right bank, lies directly opposite the city's historic center on the left bank. Also on the right bank is Catherine Mosbach's recent Bordeaux Botanical Garden (see pp. 84–89), constructed on another former industrial riverfront parcel.

In his plan for the Garonne Riverfront, Desvigne envisions a new urban park composed of large, simple spaces: long riverbanks, wide meadows, and ample woods. Promenades for pedestrians and cyclists hug the riverfront, and further inland a new parkway for motorized traffic threads through the wooded area. The detailed plan illustrates two principal phases for the growth and development of the park and its immediate surrounding industrial neighborhood. While the park loosely conforms to the riverfront, the new landscape also makes inroads perpendicular to the riverbank along the traces of former industrial lots, the existing road system, and other infrastructure elements. Some buildings remain for adaptive reuse, others are to be removed, and sites are designated for future redevelopment.

Like his Greenwich Peninsula project (see pp. 148–51), Desvigne's plan for Bordeaux is based on his idea of introducing an "intermediate landscape" of geomorphological features (encompassing natural riverbanks, marshes, meadows, and woodland environments) in order to create a landscape texture not found in the relatively barren existing conditions. Rather than mimic the traditional geometric order of the historic city's open spaces on the left bank, the organic form of the right bank will evoke a landscape that presumably existed centuries before. This approach is intended to create a naturalist landscape that will remain legible and viable and will seem as though it had always existed, long before the city was built. As a catalyst for development, Desvigne believes the aesthetic transformation of Bordeaux's right bank landscape on such a vast scale has the potential to shift the city from its traditional focus on the left bank toward a greater balance between both sides of the Garonne River.

—PR

PHOTO-COLLAGE SHOWING EXISTING CONDITIONS
OF BORDEAUX'S RIGHT BANK

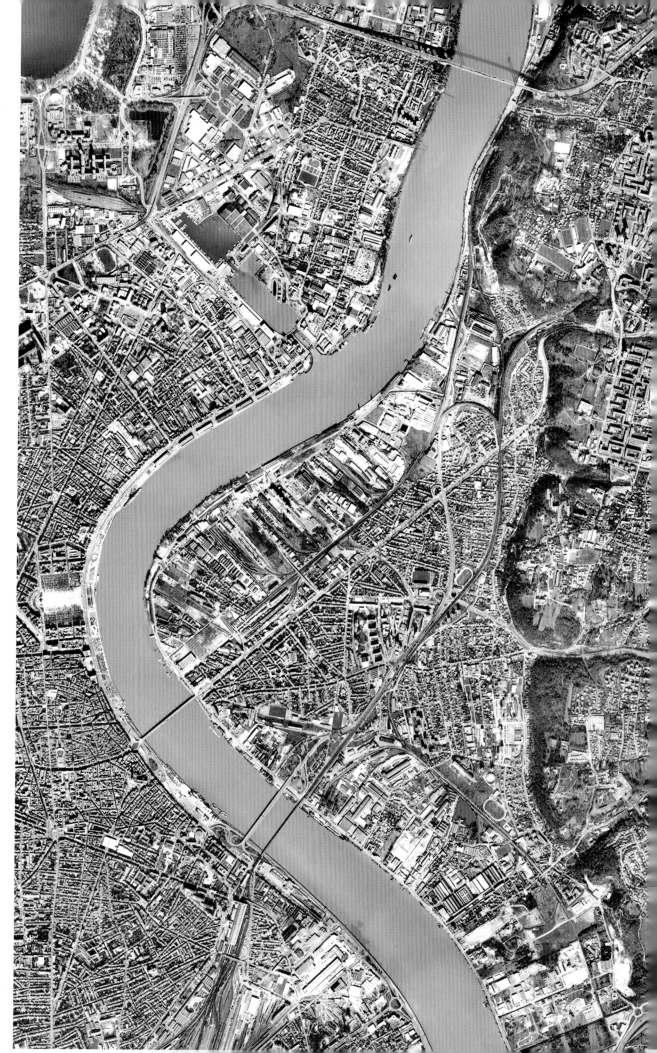

AERIAL VIEW OF BORDEAUX

LEGENDE:

PARC

LIMITE DU PARC PHASE 2

LIMITE DU PARC PHASE 1

PARC: ZONE INCONSTRUCTIBLE PHASE 2

PARC: ZONE INCONSTRUCTIBLE PHASE 1

BERGE: ZONE NATURELLE A REQUALIFIER OU A PROTEGER

RIVE ECOLOGIQUE: ESPACE NATUREL A CREER

ESPACE NATUREL A CREER

RAMIFICATION DU PARC: EQUIPEMENT DE QUARTIER / SQUARE / JARDIN

BOISEMENT

BOISEMENT A CREER

PLANTATION A CONFORTER

BÂTI

ZONE CONSTRUCTIBLE

EQUIPEMENT EXCEPTIONNEL DANS LE PARC

BÂTI EXISTANT

VOIE

VOIE A CREER

VOIRIE SECONDAIRE (PARKWAY) GABARIT: 33 M: 2x1 VOIE + STATIONNEMENT + T.P.C. PLANTE

VOIRIE TERTIAIRE (CONNECTEE AU PARKWAY) GABARIT: 12-15 M: 2x1 VOIE

VOIRIE QUATERNAIRE (DESSERTE LOCALE) GABARIT: 6 M: 1x1 VOIE

VOIE EXISTANTE

DETAIL PLAN OF RIGHT BANK

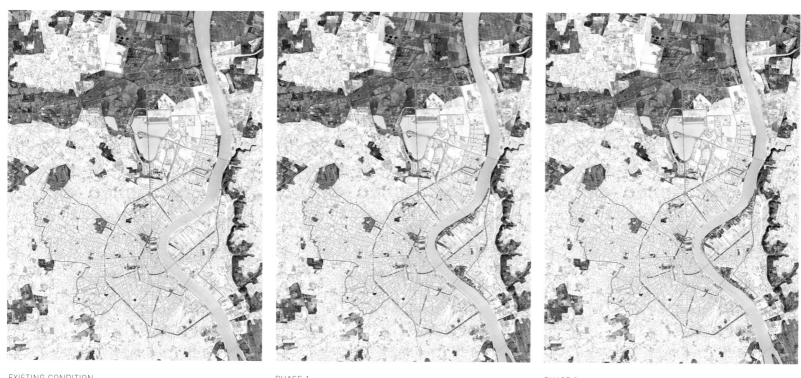

EXISTING CONDITION   PHASE 1   PHASE 2

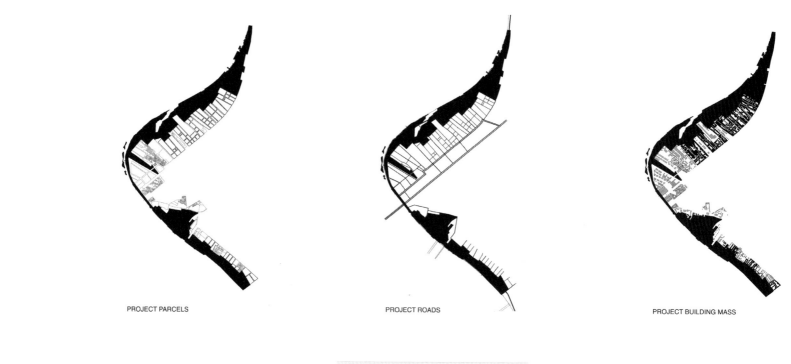

PROJECT PARCELS   PROJECT ROADS   PROJECT BUILDING MASS

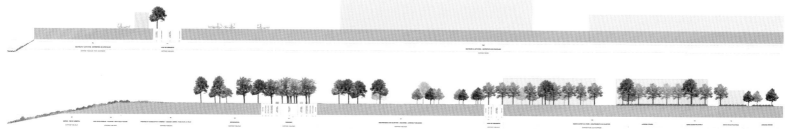

TOP: PLANS OF BORDEAUX SHOWING GREEN OPEN SPACE

MIDDLE: SITE ANALYSIS

BOTTOM: SECTIONS OF QUAI BRAZZA, BEFORE RECONSTRUCTION (ABOVE)
AND PROPOSED (BELOW)

James Corner
FIELD OPERATIONS
New York, New York

FRESH KILLS *LIFESCAPE*
Staten Island, New York 2001–05; projected start of construction, 2007

The design for the ambitious endeavor to transform New York City's Fresh Kills Landfill to parkland was awarded to Field Operations after a two-stage international competition. Rather than a fixed design, Field Operations offers a long-term strategy based on natural processes and plant life cycles to rehabilitate the severely degraded land. Of the site's 2,200 acres, nearly half are composed of creeks, wetlands, and lowland areas. Surprisingly, these areas provide a regionally significant wildlife sanctuary for migrating birds. The designers envision a rich reserve not only for wildlife, but also for cultural and social life, restoring existing marshes and forests while introducing new habitats and adding amenities for leisure and entertainment.

Fifty-three years of waste collection created an artificial topography of garbage mounds, rising to heights of 100 to 225 feet. Each mound is expected to sink unpredictably by 10 to 15 percent as its contents decompose, resulting in undulating highlands. During the composting process heat is generated, creating microclimates. Moreover, the threat of groundwater pollution and methane gas emission requires that each mound be capped with a protective polymer liner and thirty inches of soil to create an impermeable layer between the waste and the atmosphere. To chelate the soil strip cropping is proposed, an inexpensive agricultural method to improve the soil condition and to increase the soil depth. Increasing the soil's organic material inhibits metal uptake by plants, creating a more hospitable environment for plant growth. In addition, the design and implementation of localized hydraulic systems retains water on-site, supporting plant communities and preventing erosion on the mounds. These economic and environmentally sustainable techniques will remediate and revegetate the land over time.

Closed in March 2001, the landfill was unexpectedly reopened following the events of September 11. World Trade Center wreckage was transported to the west mound where law authorities and pathologists examined and collected remains. The design commemorates these events with a monumental earthwork alongside the forty-eight acre recovery site comprising two landforms the size of each tower laid upon its side.

The park will be phased in in four stages over thirty years as sections of the environment are rehabilitated. To preserve a sense of vastness, the interior of the park will remain as grasslands, while a wide and densely planted rim along the edges will provide an ecological corridor for wildlife. Programmed areas, such as recreational fields and other facilities, will be concentrated in lowland areas. New road and path systems will accommodate wildlife and pedestrian, bicycle, and vehicular traffic. Though the master plan is still to be finalized—the designs presented here are works in progress and are subject to community reviews and approval—these images capture the character and spirit of the new park.

—IS

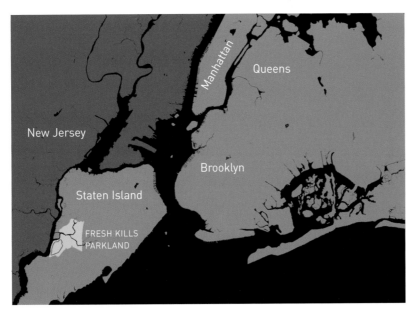

New Jersey

Manhattan

Queens

Brooklyn

Staten Island

FRESH KILLS PARKLAND

SITE CONTEXT

RENDERING OF *LIFESCAPE* FROM SOUTHEAST

VIEW OF EXISTING SITE FROM SOUTH

RENDERING OF INTERIOR OF PARK

TOP: RENDERING OF NEW LOOP DRIVE

TOP: RENDERING OF NEW WATERFRONT BOARDWALK ALONG MAIN CREEK

ABOVE: RENDERING OF NEW BOG WALK IN RESTORED SWAMP FOREST

ABOVE: RENDERING OF NEW GAME FIELDS

PROPOSED HABITAT PHASING (JULY 2004)

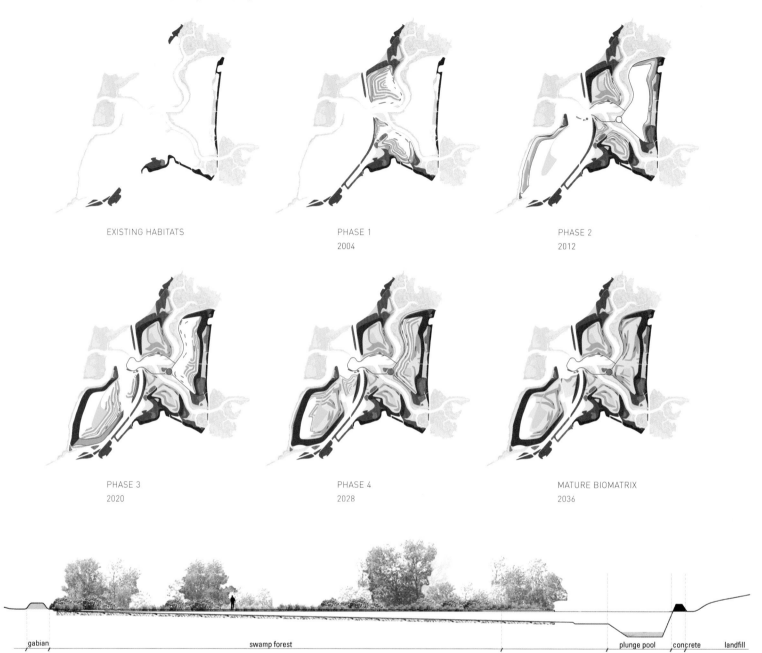

EXISTING HABITATS

PHASE 1
2004

PHASE 2
2012

PHASE 3
2020

PHASE 4
2028

MATURE BIOMATRIX
2036

gabian   swamp forest   plunge pool   concrete   landfill

LOCALIZED HYDRAULIC SYSTEM PROPOSAL: RETROFITTED STORM WATER
COLLECTION BASIN TO CREATE NEW SWAMP FOREST

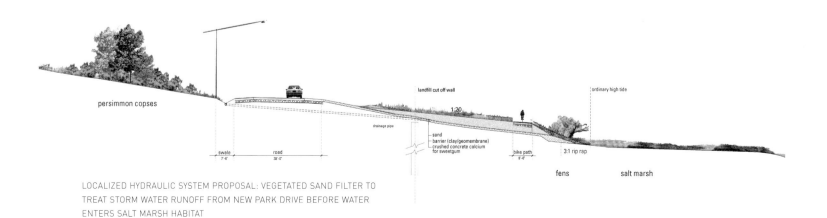

persimmon copses

landfill cut off wall

ordinary high tide

1:20

drainage pipe

sand
barrier (clay/geomembrane)
crushed concrete calcium
for sweetgum

swale   road   bike path   3:1 rip rap

fens   salt marsh

LOCALIZED HYDRAULIC SYSTEM PROPOSAL: VEGETATED SAND FILTER TO
TREAT STORM WATER RUNOFF FROM NEW PARK DRIVE BEFORE WATER
ENTERS SALT MARSH HABITAT

RENDERING OF VIEW OF MANHATTAN SKYLINE FROM
SEPTEMBER 11 EARTHWORK MONUMENT

DIAGRAM OF WEST MOUND INDICATING LOCATION OF WORLD TRADE CENTER
MATERIALS AND LANDFORMS FOR SEPTEMBER 11 EARTHWORK MONUMENT

RENDERING OF SEPTEMBER 11 EARTHWORK MONUMENT LOOK-
ING NORTHEAST

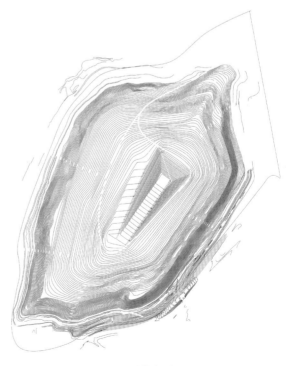

CONCEPTUAL GRADING PLAN FOR
SEPTEMBER 11 EARTH-WORK MONUMENT ON WEST MOUND

PROJECT INFORMATION

BORDEAUX BOTANICAL GARDEN
La Bastide, Bordeaux, France. 2000–02

Designer:
Catherine Mosbach, Mosbach
Paysagistes, Paris, France

Area:
11.4 acres (4.6 hectares)

Clients:
Ville de Bordeaux, Direction des Affaires
Culturelles: Philippe Richard, Conservator;
Constructions Publiques: Bernard
Dubos, Jean-Jacques Pouguet,

Design team:
Mosbach Paysagistes: N. Leroy,
Catherine Mosbach, Principal, Thi Minh
Thu N'Guyen, J. Saint-Chély, Laurence
Sciascia, Marion Talagrand (landscape
architecture); Jourda Architectes (archi-
tecture, buildings); Setec Ind: Laurent
Berger, Jean-Paul Bonroy, Emmanuel
Helme-Guizon (technical design); P.
Blanc (botany); P. Richard (botany);
Phytoconseil: J. M. David (horticulture);
R. Seroni (geology); Pascal Convert
(collaborating artist, gates)

Contractors:
Sotrap (general contractor); Bouffard
(gates); Jardins de la Brande (fencing);
Béton Projectée du Midi (stonework)

Master plan:
Agence Dominique Perrault, Paris,
France, 1992–97

**BRADFORD CITY CENTRE
MASTER PLAN**
Bradford, England. 2003; projected
completion, 2020

Designer:
Alsop Ltd, London, England

Area:
988.4 acres (400 hectares)

Client:
Bradford Centre Regeneration

Design team:
Alsop Ltd: James Allen, William Alsop,
Principal, Mark Boyce, Nick Browne,
Julia Feix, Kathryn Larriva, Capucine
Lasen, Andy Lebisch, Laurie Peake,
Bridget Sawyers, King Sturge, Stephen
Swain, Atam Verdi, David West, Project
Director (urban design and planning);
IDC Ltd: Ian Woodward (real estate and
property analysis); New Economics
Foundation: Peter Ramsden, John Taylor
(economic development); Mainstreet
Advisors: Jody Tablesporter (economic
development); Peter Brett Associates:
Richard Latcham, Tony Sheach (traffic
and transportation); Davis Langdon:
Stephen Frood (cost estimation); Elmwood:
Jan Hirst, Simon Preece, Jon Stubley,
Eric Sui (branding); Simon Mountford
Communications: Simon Mountford
(branding); A Models: Christian Spencer
Davies, Sally Spencer Davies (models);
Squint Opera: Oliver Alsop, Jules Cocke,
Martin Hampton, Isambard Khroustaliov,
Dean Koonjul, Alice Scott (film)

CRISSY FIELD
PRESIDIO NATIONAL PARK
San Francisco, California. 1994–2001

Designer:
Hargreaves Associates, San Francisco,
California, and Cambridge,
Massachusetts

Area:
100 acres (40.5 hectares)

Client:
Golden Gate National Parks Conservancy

Owner:
National Parks Service

Design team:
Hargreaves Associates: George
Hargreaves, Senior Principal, Mary
Margaret Jones, Senior Principal,
Catherine Miller, Kirt Rieder (landscape
architecture and planning); Moffatt &
Nichol Engineers (civil and marine engi-
neering); EGH Associates (structural
engineering, bridge); Philip Williams &
Associates (hydraulic design, wetlands);
Rana Creek Restoration (grass and
plants research); Wetland Research
Associates (wetlands plants); Leddy
Maytum Stacy (architecture)

Contractor:
Ghilotti Brothers Construction, Inc.

**DUISBURG-NORD
LANDSCAPE PARK**
**International Building Exhibition (IBA)
Emscher Park**
Duisburg, Germany. 1990–2002

Designer:
Peter Latz, Latz + Partner, Kranzberg,
Germany

Area:
568.3 acres (230 hectares)

Clients:
Landesentwicklungsgesellschaft
Nordrhein – Westfalen LEG NRW als
Treuhänder der Stadt Duisburg;
Emschergenossenschaft Essen;
Kommunalverband Ruhrgebiet KVR
Essen

Design team:
Latz + Partner: Peter Latz with Karl-Heinz Danielzik, Christine Rupp-Stoppel (landscape architecture); Günter Lipkowsky (architecture, buildings); Latz – Riehl: Claus Heimann, Wigbert Riehl (construction administration); Soil Remediation + Recycling GmbH BSR: W. Fahrner (soil remediation); Planning Office Dittrich (structural engineering, elevated walkway in sintering bunkers); Rothe Engineers (structural engineering, bridges and constructions in the new canal); Korte + Greiwe Engineers (engineering, clarification of preconditions); Pecher Engineers (engineering, subterranean sewer); Prof. Schatter (wind energy, windmill); Prof. Fröhlich (engineering, windmill, dynamic forces); Rothe Engineers, Essen (engineering, windmill, statics); Prof. Harnach Engineers (engineering, statics, footbridge in ore bunker gallery, stabilization of concrete walls); Prof. Jörg Dettmar (botany); Jonathan Park (lighting, blast furnace)

Volunteer and community groups:
IG Nordpark, Gesellschaft für Industriekultur

EXCHANGE SQUARE
Manchester, England. 1998–2000

Designer:
Martha Schwartz, Martha Schwartz, Inc., Cambridge, Massachusetts

Area:
2.5 acres (1 hectare)

Client:
Manchester Millennium Ltd

Design team:
Martha Schwartz, Inc.: Tricia Bales, Evelyn Bergaila, Scott Carmen, Lital Fabian, Shauna Gillies-Smith, Senior Project Designer, Raphael Justewicz, Paula Meijerink, Wes Michaels, Martha Schwartz, Principal, Don Sharp (landscape architecture); Michael Blier (perspective renderings)

Associate architect and engineer:
Urban Solutions, Manchester, England: James Chapman

Master plan:
EDAW, London, England, 1996–present

FRESH KILLS *LIFESCAPE*
Staten Island, New York. 2001–05; projected start of construction, 2007

Designer:
James Corner, Field Operations, New York, New York

Area:
2,200 acres (890 hectares)

Client:
New York City Department of City Planning

Sponsors:
New York City Department of Sanitation, New York City Department of Cultural Affairs, New York City Department of Parks and Recreation, New York City Department of Transportation, Office of the Staten Island Borough President, New York State Department of State, New York State Department of Environmental Conservation, New York State Department of Transportation, Municipal Art Society

Design team:
Field Operations: James Corner, Principal, Michael Flynn, Brian Goldberg, Justine Heilner, Nahyun Hwang, Tom Jost, Project Manager, Te Hsuan Liao, Ellen Neises, Design Project Manager, Lisa Switkin (landscape architecture and urban design); Allee, King, Rosen & Fleming (environmental planning); Stan Allen Architect (architecture); ARUP (transportation engineering); Applied Ecological Services (ecological restoration); Curry & Kerlinger (avian ecology); GeoSyntec (landfill engineering); Hamilton, Rabinovitz & Alschuler (outreach and financial planning); L'Observatoire International (lighting); Richard Lynch (natural systems and plant ecology); Skidmore, Owings & Merrill LLP (urban design and planning); Tomato (media arts and communications); Mierle Laderman Ukeles (Percent for Art artist)

GARONNE RIVERFRONT MASTER PLAN
Bordeaux, France. 2003–04; projected completion, 2034

Designer:
Michel Desvigne, Paris, France

Area:
334 acres (135.2 hectares)

Client:
Ville de Bordeaux

Design team:
Ana Marti-Baron, Luc Chignier, Michel Desvigne, Principal, Sophie Mourthé, Project Manager (landscape architecture and planning)

GREENWICH PENINSULA
London, England. 1997–2000 (partially realized)

Designer:
Michel Desvigne, Desvigne & Dalnoky, Paris, France

Area:
49.4 acres (20 hectares)

Client:
English Partnerships

Design team:
Desvigne & Dalnoky: Michel Desvigne, Principal, Giovanna Vallardi, Pauline Way, Project Manager (landscape architecture); WS Atkins Ltd (landscape architecture and engineering)

Associate landscape architect:
Bernard Ede, Bath, England

Master plan:
Richard Rogers Partnership, London, England, 1996–2000

HADIQAT AS-SAMAH
(Garden of Forgiveness)
Beirut Central District, Beirut, Lebanon. 2000; projected completion, 2006

Designers:
Kathryn Gustafson and Neil Porter, Gustafson Porter Ltd, London, England

Area:
5.7 acres (2.3 hectares)

Client:
Solidere, The Lebanese Company for the Development and Reconstruction of Beirut Central District, s.a.l.

Design team:
Gustafson Porter Ltd: Neil Black, Frances Christie, Paula Craft, Kathryn Gustafson, Director, Nick Hughes, Max Norman, Nilesh Patel, Neil Porter, Director, Gerardo Puente, Jose Rosa, Julia Wessendorf (landscape architecture and architecture); ARUP: Ian Carradice, Nick Jeffries (engineering, schematic design); Richard Hughes (archaeology, schematic design); Dar Al-Handasah: Joyce Inglessis, Suhail Srour (engineering, construction); Yaser Abun-Nasr Architects (archaeology conservation); Historic Lebanon: Sami el-Masri (archaeology conservation); Muntaha Saghieh Beydoun (site archaeology); Hans Curvers (site archaeology)

IGUALADA CEMETERY PARK
Igualada, Spain. 1985–96 (partially completed)

Designers:
Enric Miralles and Carme Pinós, Barcelona, Spain

Area:
3.5 acres (1.4 hectares)

Client:
Ayuntamiento de Igualada

Design team:
Enric Miralles and Carme Pinós with Joan Callis, Se Duch, Albert Ferre, Josep Mias, Eva Prats (architecture and site design); Jordi Altés (technical design); Robert Brufau (structural engineering); Agustí Obiols (structural engineering)

INVALIDENPARK
Berlin, Germany. 1992–97

Designers:
Christophe Girot, Atelier Phusis, Paris, France

Area:
4.5 acres (1.8 hectares)

Clients:
Stadtgrün Berlin; Bundesgartenschau Berlin 1995 Park GmbH; Berlin Senatsverwaltung für Stadtentwicklung und Umweltschutz

Design team:
Atelier Phusis: Jean Marc L'Anton, Partner, Leonor Cheis de Sousa, Marc Claramunt, Partner, Christophe Girot, Partner, Alain Goldtsimmer, Claudia Grasshoff, Dominique Hernandez, Project Coordinator, Anja Morsch, Christine Wieskotten (landscape architecture); Frank Neau (perspective renderings); Dusapin et Leclercq (architecture and planning); Marc Mimram (engineering); Hallman und Rohn AG: Horst Schumacher (technical drawings); Onne: Christophe Girot (construction administration); PALA AG: Herr Fromm (civil engineering and construction management); L'Observatoire 1 (lighting)

KEYAKI PLAZA
SAITAMA NEW URBAN CENTER
Saitama City, Japan. 1994–2000

Designers:
Yoji Sasaki, OHTORI Consultants Environmental Design Institute, Osaka, Japan; Peter Walker, Peter Walker William Johnson and Partners, Berkeley, California; Masayuki Kusumoto, NTT Urban Development Co., Tokyo, Japan

Area:
2.7 acres (1.1 hectares)

Client:
Saitama Prefecture Government

Design team:
OHTORI Consultants: Koshi Iwata, Nobutaka Nagahama, Yoji Sasaki, Principal (landscape architecture); Peter Walker William Johnson and Partners: Doug Findlay, William Johnson, Partner, Ken Kawai, Hiko Mitani, David Walker, Peter Walker, Partner (landscape architecture); NTT Urban Development Co.: Masayuki Kusumoto, Tomoyuki Sakaue (architecture); TIS & Partners (structural engineering); Kume Sekkei (structural engineering); Lighting Planners Associates (lighting)

Contractors:
Nishimatsu (architecture); Sumitomo (architecture); Ageo and Hassei (joint venture, architecture); Kofuen (landscape planting); Uekaku and Imai (joint venture, landscape planting); Angyo (landscape planting); Yokoyama and Susuki (joint venture, landscape planting)

LURIE GARDEN
MILLENNIUM PARK
Chicago, Illinois. 2000–04

Designers:
Kathryn Gustafson, Gustafson Guthrie Nichol Ltd., Seattle, Washington; Piet Oudolf, Hummelo, the Netherlands; Robert Israel, Robert Israel, Inc., Los Angeles, California

Area:
3 acres (1.2 hectares)

Client:
Millennium Park Inc.

Client representatives:
Edward Uhlir, Assistant to the Mayor and Project Director; David Troszak, Spectrum Strategies

Design team:
Gustafson Guthrie Nichol Ltd.: Rodrigo Abela, Kathryn Gustafson, Senior Design Partner, Jennifer Guthrie, Managing Partner, Gareth Loveridge, Project Architect, David Nelson, Shannon Nichol, Design Partner (landscape architecture); Piet Oudolf (perennial planting); Robert Israel, Inc.: Robert Israel (conceptual consulting); KPFF Consulting Engineers (structural and civil engineering); EME, LLC (electrical and mechanical engineering); CMS Collaborative (fountain engineering); Jeffrey L. Bruce & Company LLC (irrigation design); Schuler & Shook, Inc. (lighting); ArchiTech (specifications); Davis Langdon Adamson (cost estimation)

Associate landscape architect:
Terry Guen Design Associates, Inc., Chicago, Illinois

Contractor:
Walsh Construction

Master plan:
Skidmore, Owings & Merrill LLP, Chicago, Illinois, 1998–2001

MANCHESTER CITY CENTRE MASTER PLAN
Manchester, England. 1996–present

Designer:
EDAW, London, England

Area:
61.8 acres (25 hectares)

Clients:
Manchester Millennium Ltd; Manchester City Council

Design team:
EDAW: Joanna Averley, David Cox, Paula Garvey, Bill Hanway, Peter Neal, Jason Prior, Regional Director and Vice President, Mick Timpson (planning and design coordination); Oscar Faber (transportation consulting); Ian Simpson Architects (master plan consulting); Benoy (retail strategy); Alan Baxter & Associates (infrastructure); Building Design Partnership (master plan consulting); MACE (program management); Davis Langdon Everest (quantity survey)

THE MUSEUM OF MODERN ART ROOF GARDEN
New York, New York. 2003–05

Designer:
Ken Smith, Ken Smith Landscape Architect, New York, New York

Area:
North Roof: 10,200 sq. ft. (947.6 sq. m); South Roof: 7,200 sq. ft. (668.9 sq. m)

Client:
The Museum of Modern Art

Design team:
Ken Smith Landscape Architect: Tobias Armborst, Elizabeth Asawa, David Hamerman, Matt Landis, Rocio Lastras, Ken Smith, Principal, Judith Wong, Christian Zimmermann (landscape architecture)

Contractor:
Town and Gardens

NORTHEAST COASTAL PARK
Forum 2004
Barcelona, Spain. 2000–04

Designer:
Abalos & Herreros, Madrid, Spain

Area:
44 acres (17.8 hectares)

Client:
Infraestructures 2004; Área de Manteniment i Serveis, Ajuntament de Barcelona

Design team:
Abalos & Herreros: Iñaki Abalos, Juan Herreros, Renata Sentkiewicz with Juan J. González, Pablo Martínez Capdevila, Mario Pascual, Pablo Puertas, David Sobrino, Roger Subirá, Wouter van Daele, Irene Zúñiga (site design and architecture); Albert Oehlen (collaborating artist); Obiol, Moya y Asociados SL (structural engineering); PGI Group (mechanical engineering and installations); Bet Figueras (horticulture); José Maria Civit (lighting); Carles Teixidó (project management)

Contractors:
ACS (park); CESPA (planting); UTE (CESPA+EMT+TERSA+URBASER) (buildings); Acieroid (metal structures); Escofet (Xurret seating system); Santa y Cole (pep line)

OLYMPIC SCULPTURE PARK
Seattle Art Museum
Seattle, Washington. 2001; projected completion, 2006

Designer:
Weiss/Manfredi Architects, New York, New York

Area:
8.5 acres (3.4 hectares)

Client:
Seattle Art Museum: Mimi Gardner Gates, Director; Chris Rogers, Director of Capital Projects; Lisa Corrin, Deputy Director of Art

Design team:
Weiss/Manfredi Architects: Christopher Ballentine, Project Manager, Michael Blasberg, Lauren Crahan, Kok Kian Goh, Mike Harshman, Todd Hoehn, Project Architect, Mustapha Jundi, Justin Kwok, Michael Manfredi, Design Partner, John Peek, Project Architect, Yehre Suh, Project Architect, Akari Takebayashi, Design Partner, Marion Weiss, Design Partner (site design and architecture); Magnusson Klemencic Associates: Drew Gangnes, Rita Greene, Lavina Sadhwani, Jay Taylor (civil and structural engineering); Charles Anderson Landscape Architecture: Charles Anderson, Julie Parrett (landscape architecture); Brandston Partnership, Inc.: Chou Lien, Burr Rutledge (lighting); Hart-Crowser, Inc.: John Bingham, Garry Horvitz (geotechnical engineering); Anchor Environmental: Peter Hummel, Tracey McKenzie (aquatic science engineering); Aspect Consulting: Laurie Herman (environmental engineering); Abacus Engineered Systems: Greg Livengood, Mark Stavig (mechanical electrical plumbing fire-proofing engineering); Pentagram: Abbott Miller, Lisa Strausfeld (graphic design); Barrientos, LLC (project management)

Construction management and contractor:
Sellen Construction

PARC DE LA COUR DU MAROC
Paris, France. 2003; projected completion, 2006

Designers:
Michel and Claire Corajoud, Paris, France; ADR and Georges Descombes, Geneva, Switzerland

Area:
10.7 acres (4.3 hectares)

Client:
Ville de Paris

Design team:
Michel and Claire Corajoud with Arnaud Alatissiere, Yannick Salliot (landscape architecture); ADR: Julien Descombes, Marco Rampini with Greg Bussien, Vincent Manzoni (architecture); Georges Descombes (site design and architecture); Philippe Cointault (perspective renderings); AEP Normand (engineering); ECERP (engineering); Les Eclairagistes Associés (lighting); JFL Concept (irrigation); Jean-Max Llorrca (fountain engineering); Techingenierie (engineering); Stéphane Tonnelat (sociology); Yann Renaud (sociology); Gabriel Chauvel (landscape design); Carmen Perrin (artist)

PICCADILLY GARDENS
Manchester, England. 1998–2002

Designers:
ARUP, Manchester, England; EDAW, London, England

Area:
13.6 acres (5.5 hectares)

Client:
Manchester City Council

Design team:
ARUP: Michael Marr, Roger Milburn, Richard Summers (engineering); EDAW: Jim Chapman, Christopher Elliott, Paula Garvey, Peter Neal, Warren Osborne, Jason Prior, Regional Director and Vice President (landscape architecture); Tadao Ando Architect and Associates (architecture, pavilion); Art2Architecture: Peter Fink (lighting); Davis Langdon Everest (quantity survey); Shepherd Gilmour (planning supervision)

Associate architect:
Chapman Robinson Architects,
Manchester, England

Contractor:
Balfour Beatty Civil Engineering Ltd

Master plan:
EDAW, London, England, 1996–present

SCHOUWBURGPLEIN
(Theater Square)
Rotterdam, the Netherlands. 1991–96

Designer:
Adriaan Geuze, West 8 urban design &
landscape architecture bv, Rotterdam,
the Netherlands

Area:
3 acres (1.2 hectares)

Client:
Gemeente Rotterdam

Design team:
West 8 urban design & landscape archi-
tecture bv: Jurgen Beij, Erwin Bot, Cyrus
B. Clark, Dirry de Bruin, Adriaan Geuze,
Principal, Dick Heydra, Huub Juurlink,
Wim Kloosterboer, Erik Overdiep, Nigel
Sampey, Jerry van Eyck (landscape
architecture and urban design); Duyvis
BV: Koog aan de Zaan (engineering,
hydraulic light mast sculpture)

SHANGHAI CARPET
SHANGHAI YANG PU UNIVERSITY
CITY HUB
Shanghai, China. 2003; projected
completion, 2006

Designers:
Tom Leader, Tom Leader Studio,
Berkeley, California; Michael Duncan,
Skidmore, Owings & Merrill LLP,
San Francisco, California

Area:
14.6 acres (5.9 hectares)

Client:
Shui On Properties Ltd.

Design team:
Tom Leader Studio: Philippe Coignet,
Tom Leader, Ryosuke Shimoda (land-
scape architecture); Skidmore, Owings &
Merrill LLP: Toby Bath, Larry Chien,
Erica Deitchman, Michael Duncan, Design
Associate Partner, Frank Grima, Lara
Kaufman, Sean Kennedy, John Kriken,
Consulting Partner, Ellen Lou, Planning
Associate Partner, William Marvez, Tom
McMillan, Masis Mesropian, Eric Osth,
Benjamin Parco, Soo Youn Park, Anne
Poon, Sean Ragasa, Champaka Rajagopal,
Ganesh Ramachandran, Randy Ruiz,
Gene Schnair, Managing Partner, Sandra
Speer, Henry Vlanin, Jodi Weinstein,
Andrea Wong, James Yan, Patricia Yeh
(architecture, planning, project manage-
ment, structural engineering, mechanical,
electrical, and plumbing engineering);
Water Architecture: Dan Euser (fountain
engineering); Shen Milsom Wilke (audio-
visual); Proces2: Sean Ahlquist (illustra-
tion); Ratio Design (models)

Associate architect:
P & T Group, Shanghai, China

Associate landscape architect:
Design Land Cooperative

SHELL PETROLEUM
HEADQUARTERS
Rueil-Malmaison, France. 1989–91

Designers:
Kathryn Gustafson, Paysage Land, Paris,
France; Valode & Pistre Architectes,
Paris, France

Area:
6.2 acres (2.5 hectares)

Client:
Shell Petroleum

Design team:
Paysage Land: Kathryn Gustafson with
Karl Brugmann, Sylvie Farges, Melissa
Brown Lacoast (landscape architecture);
Valode & Pistre Architectes: Denis
Valode (architecture)

Contractor:
Moser (landscape installation)

SOUTHEAST COASTAL PARK
Forum 2004
Barcelona, Spain. 2000–04

Designers:
Farshid Moussavi and Alejandro
Zaera-Polo, Foreign Office Architects,
London, England

Area:
12.4 acres (5 hectares)

Clients:
Infraestructures 2004; Área de
Manteniment i Serveis, Ajuntament de
Barcelona

Design team:
Foreign Office Architects: Niccoló Cadeo,
Danielle Domeniconi, Juanjo González,
Marco Guarnieri, Sergio López-Piñeiro,
Farshid Moussavi, Principal, Pablo Ros,
Terence Seah, Daniel Valle, Lluís Viú
Rebes, Alejandro Zaera-Polo, Principal
(site design and architecture); Obiol,
Moya y Asociados SL (structural engi-
neering); Teresa Galí (landscape archi-
tecture); Proisotec (mechanical and
electrical engineering); Tg3 (quantity
survey); BCN (quantity survey); A Models
(models)

CREDITS

In reproducing the images contained in this publication, every effort has been made to obtain the permission of the rights holders. In any instances where the Museum could not locate the rights holders, notwithstanding good faith efforts, it requests that any contact information concerning such rights holders be forwarded, so that they may be contacted for future editions. All drawings and renderings related to the projects are copyright to their respective designers unless otherwise indicated.

Abalos & Herreros: 144, 145; ADR and Georges Descombes: 138; Albatross Aerial Photography Ltd./Duby Tal: 29 (right); Alsop & Partners and Bradford Center Regeneration: 52–57; Argent Group PLC: 50 (bottom left); Atelier 17/Christa Panick: 5 (top left), 125, 128 (bottom), 131 (top); Gabriele Basilico: 21 (right); Michael Blier: 43 (top); Luc Boegly: 6 (top), 91, 92, 94, 95; Burle Marx & Cia Ltda/Haruyoshi Ono: 22 (top); Chamois Moon/Robert Campbell: 133; Michel Desvigne: 152, 153; Desvigne & Dalnoky, courtesy of Michel Desvigne: 10; Antonio Duharte, courtesy of Michel Desvigne: 30 (bottom); © 1999 EDAW: 51 (bottom left); EDAW/© 2002 Dixi Carillo: 4 (right), 49, 50 (top left), 51 (top, bottom right); EDAW/© 2004 Dixi Carillo: 50 (top right); EDAW and Cities Revealed® aerial photography, © 1995 The Geoinformation® Group: 41 (left); EDAW/aerial image courtesy of UKperspectives.com: 41 (right); Field Operations: 5 (bottom left), 31 (bottom); Foreign Office Architects: 103, 107; Frederick Law Olmstead National Historic Site, courtesy of Marion Pressley, Pressley Associates, Inc.: 31 (top); Courtesy of Bryan Fuermann: 26 (top left); Shauna Gilles-Smith: 47;

Christophe Girot: 5 (right), 71–73; Golden Gate National Parks Conservancy: 134 (top left, center left); John Gollings: 27 (right), 28 (left), 137 (bottom left, bottom right); Len Grant: 44 (left), 46 (left, bottom right); Gustafson Porter Ltd: 74, 76; Hargreaves Associates: 4 (top left), 132, 134 (bottom left, center right), 136; Hedrich Blessing Photography/Scott McDonald: 100 (top), 101; The Estate of Kazuaki Hosokawa: 6 (bottom), 59 (bottom), 60 (top left), 62 (bottom), 63 (right); IBA Emscher Park GmbH: 26 (top); Markus Jatsch, courtesy of Martha Schwartz: 27 (left); Landesarchiv Berlin: 70 (left); Landesluftbildarchiv, Senatsverwaltung für Stadtentwicklung: 70 (right); Michael Latz: 126 (top), 128 (top left), 130 (top right, center, bottom), 131 (center left, center right); Peter Liedtke: 128 (top right); Duccio Malagamba: 3, 111 (top), 114, 115 (top right); Manchester City Council, courtesy of EDAW, London: 40 (right); Martha Schwartz, Inc.: 43 (bottom); Bill Miller: 50 (bottom right); Mosbach Paysagistes/ P. Ecoutin: 87 (top left, bottom right); Mosbach Paysagistes/Catherine Mosbach: 85, 87 (bottom left, top right), 88, 89; Jeroen Musch: 7, 34 (top), 35, 37–39; The Museum of Modern Art, New York: 19 (right), 22 (bottom); News Team International Limited: 40 (left); OHTORI Consultants Environmental Design Institute: 20 (bottom); Koji Okumura: 63 (left); Paul Mellon Collection, Yale Center for British Art: 14, 15; Peter Walker and Partners: 60 (bottom), 61; Peter Walker and Partners/David Walker: 20 (top); Carme Pinós and the Estate of Enric Miralles, courtesy of Enric Miralles Benedetta Tagliabue Arquitectes Associats: 110, 112; Mary Randlett: 25; Peter Reed: 26 (bottom left), 30 (top), 111 (bottom), 131 (bottom left); Chris

Roberts: 97; Cervin Robinson: 19 (left); Saitama Prefecture: 58 (right); David Sanger: 134 (top right, bottom right), 135 (bottom), 137 (top); Yoji Sasaki: 58 (left); Martha Schwartz: 44 (right), 46 (top right); Seattle Art Museum: 117 (left); Simmons Aerofilms Limited: 48, 149; Skidmore, Owings & Merrill LLP, Chicago: 96; Skidmore, Owings & Merrill LLP, San Francisco: 64, 65, 69; Skidmore, Owings & Merrill LLP, San Francisco/Michael Duncan: 21 (left); Solidere s.a.l. Societé Libanaise pour le Developpement et la Reconstruction du Centre-ville de Beyrouth (The Lebanese Company for the Development and Reconstruction of Beirut Central District): 78 (right); Hisao Suzuki: 28 (right), 113, 115 (top left, bottom); Lital Szmuk, courtesy of Martha Schwartz: 29 (left); Hiroshi Tanaka: 59 (top), 60 (top right, center), 62 (top); ThyssenKrupp AG, courtesy of Latz + Partner: 124 (bottom); Tom Leader Studio: 4 (bottom left), 66–68; Manfred Vollmer: 124 (top); Stephen Vos: 139; Alan Ward: 45; Webster & Stevens, courtesy of PEMCO Webster & Stevens Collection, Museum of History & Industry, Seattle: 24 (top); Weiss/Manfredi Architects: 24 (bottom), 116; Daniel Willner: 82 (top); © 1990 Adam Woolfitt: 148; Harf Zimmermann: 129, 130 (top left)

Front cover:
Clockwise from top left: Mosbach Paysagistes/Catherine Mosbach; Martha Schwartz; Atelier 17/Christa Panick; Luc Boegly; David Sanger; Jeroen Musch

Back cover:
Clockwise from top left: Field Operations; Jeroen Musch; Yoji Sasaki; Tom Leader Studio